The Secrets of Successful Entrepreneurs

Strategies for Building a Thriving Business

By

Writen

Lawal kola

Book Cover by [kola lawal]

Illustrations by [lawal kola]

[Edition 3] edition [2023]

TABLE OF CONTENT

---

[1]

Chapter 1
The Mindset of Successful Entrepreneurs

In order to achieve success as an entrepreneur, it is crucial to develop the right mindset. The way we think and perceive the world greatly influences our actions and decisions. In this chapter, we will explore the mindset of successful entrepreneurs and the key strategies they employ to build thriving businesses. From developing a growth mindset to overcoming fear and failure, cultivating resilience, embracing change and adaptability, setting clear goals and vision, and building confidence and self-belief, we will delve into the mindset shifts that can propel entrepreneurs towards success. By understanding and adopting the mindset of successful entrepreneurs, you will be equipped with the tools and strategies necessary to navigate the challenges and uncertainties of entrepreneurship and build a business that thrives

Section 1.1
Developing a Growth Mindset

Developing a growth mindset is a crucial aspect of becoming a successful entrepreneur. A growth mindset is the belief that abilities and intelligence can be developed through dedication, hard work, and continuous learning. It is the opposite of a fixed mindset, which believes that abilities and intelligence are fixed traits that cannot be changed.

Entrepreneurs with a growth mindset are more likely to embrace challenges and see them as opportunities for growth. They are not afraid of failure, but rather view it as a stepping stone towards success. They understand that setbacks and obstacles are part of the entrepreneurial journey and use them as learning experiences.

To develop a growth mindset, it is important to start by recognizing and challenging any fixed beliefs or negative self-talk that may be holding you back. Replace thoughts like "I'm not good enough"or "I can't do this"with more positive and empowering beliefs such as "I can learn and improve"or "I am capable of overcoming challenges."

Another key aspect of developing a growth mindset is embracing a love for learning. Successful entrepreneurs are constantly seeking new knowledge and skills to improve themselves and their businesses. They understand that learning is a lifelong process and are open to new ideas and perspectives.

It is also important to surround yourself with like-minded individuals who support and encourage your growth. Seek out mentors, join entrepreneurial communities, and engage in networking opportunities to connect with others who share your mindset and can provide guidance and support.

In addition, practicing resilience is essential for developing a growth mindset. Resilience is the ability to bounce back from setbacks and keep moving forward. It involves staying positive, staying focused on your goals, and not letting failures or setbacks define you.

Finally, developing a growth mindset requires a willingness to step out of your comfort zone and take calculated risks. Successful entrepreneurs understand that growth and success often come from pushing boundaries and trying new things. They are not afraid to take risks and are willing to learn from both successes and failures.

Section 1.2
Overcoming Fear and Failure

Fear and failure are two common obstacles that entrepreneurs face on their journey to success. However, successful entrepreneurs understand that these challenges are not roadblocks, but rather opportunities for growth and learning. They have developed strategies to overcome fear and failure, allowing them to move forward with confidence and resilience.

One key strategy for overcoming fear is to reframe it as excitement. Instead of viewing fear as a negative emotion that holds them back, successful entrepreneurs see it as a sign that they are stepping outside of their comfort zone and pushing themselves to grow. They embrace the feeling of excitement that comes with taking risks and view failure as a necessary part of the learning process.

Another important aspect of overcoming fear and failure is developing a strong support system. Successful entrepreneurs surround themselves with like-minded individuals who understand the challenges they face and can provide guidance and encouragement. They seek out mentors and join networking groups to connect with others who have experienced similar struggles and can offer valuable insights.

Additionally, successful entrepreneurs understand the importance of self-belief and positive self-talk. They recognize that their mindset plays a crucial role in their ability to overcome fear and failure. They practice affirmations and visualization techniques to build confidence and maintain a positive outlook, even in the face of setbacks.

Furthermore, successful entrepreneurs embrace failure as a learning opportunity. They understand that failure is not a reflection of their worth or abilities, but rather a chance to learn from their mistakes and improve. They analyze their failures, identify the lessons learned, and use that knowledge to make better decisions in the future.

Lastly, successful entrepreneurs maintain a growth mindset. They view challenges and setbacks as opportunities for personal and professional development. They constantly seek out new knowledge and skills, and they are not afraid to take calculated risks. They understand that failure is not the end, but rather a stepping stone towards success.

In conclusion, overcoming fear and failure is a crucial aspect of the mindset of successful entrepreneurs. By reframing fear as excitement, building a strong support system, practicing positive self-talk, embracing failure as a learning opportunity, and maintaining a growth mindset, entrepreneurs can overcome these obstacles and continue on their path to success.

In conclusion, developing a growth mindset is a fundamental aspect of becoming a successful entrepreneur. It involves challenging fixed beliefs, embracing a love for learning, surrounding yourself with supportive individuals, practicing resilience, and taking calculated risks. By cultivating a growth mindset, you can unlock your full potential and achieve greater success in your entrepreneurial journey.

Section 1.3
Cultivating Resilience

Resilience is a crucial trait for any successful entrepreneur. It is the ability to bounce back from setbacks, adapt to challenges, and persevere in the face of adversity. Cultivating resilience is essential because entrepreneurship is filled with ups and downs, and being able to navigate through the tough times is what sets successful entrepreneurs apart.

One way to cultivate resilience is by developing a positive mindset. This involves reframing setbacks as learning opportunities and focusing on solutions rather than dwelling on problems. By maintaining a positive outlook, entrepreneurs can approach challenges with a sense of optimism and determination.

Another important aspect of cultivating resilience is building a strong support network. Surrounding yourself with like-minded individuals who understand the entrepreneurial journey can provide valuable emotional support and guidance. This network can include mentors, fellow entrepreneurs, or even friends and family who believe in your vision and can offer encouragement during difficult times.

Additionally, practicing self-care is crucial for building resilience. Taking care of your physical and mental well-being allows you to recharge and maintain a clear perspective. This can include activities such as exercise, meditation, getting enough sleep, and engaging in hobbies or activities that bring you joy and relaxation.

Resilient entrepreneurs also understand the importance of embracing failure as a stepping stone to success. Rather than viewing failure as a setback, they see it as an opportunity to learn, grow, and improve. By reframing failure in this way, entrepreneurs can bounce back stronger and more determined than ever.

Furthermore, cultivating resilience involves being adaptable and flexible in the face of change. The business landscape is constantly evolving, and successful entrepreneurs are able to pivot and adjust their strategies accordingly. This may involve embracing new technologies, exploring different markets, or even reinventing their business model to stay relevant and competitive.

Lastly, celebrating small wins along the way is essential

for maintaining resilience. Acknowledging and appreciating progress, no matter how small, can boost motivation and confidence. By recognizing and celebrating achievements, entrepreneurs can stay motivated and inspired to continue pushing forward.

In conclusion, cultivating resilience is a vital aspect of the mindset of successful entrepreneurs. By developing a positive mindset, building a strong support network, practicing self-care, embracing failure, being adaptable, and celebrating small wins, entrepreneurs can navigate through challenges and setbacks with resilience and ultimately build a thriving business.

Section 1.4
Embracing Change and Adaptability

Change is an inevitable part of life, and this holds true for the world of entrepreneurship as well. Successful entrepreneurs understand that in order to thrive in a constantly evolving business landscape, they must embrace change and adaptability. They recognize that clinging to outdated strategies and resisting change can hinder their growth and limit their potential for success.

Embracing change means being open to new ideas, technologies, and market trends. It requires a willingness to step out of your comfort zone and explore new possibilities. Successful entrepreneurs understand that change can bring about opportunities for innovation and growth. They actively seek out ways to stay ahead of the curve and adapt their business strategies to meet the changing needs and demands of their customers.

Adaptability is closely linked to embracing change. It is the ability to adjust and modify your approach in response to new circumstances or challenges. Successful entrepreneurs understand that what worked in the past may not necessarily work in the future. They are willing to pivot their business strategies and make necessary adjustments to stay relevant and competitive. One key aspect of embracing change and adaptability is having a growth mindset. This mindset is characterized by a belief that abilities and intelligence can be developed through dedication and hard work. It is the opposite of a fixed mindset, which believes that abilities are fixed and cannot be changed. Successful entrepreneurs with a growth mindset see challenges as opportunities for learning and growth. They view setbacks as temporary and use them as stepping stones to future success.

Another important factor in embracing change and adaptability is being proactive rather than reactive. Successful entrepreneurs actively seek out new information, trends, and technologies that can impact their industry. They stay informed about market shifts and customer preferences, and they are quick to adapt their strategies accordingly. They are not afraid to take calculated risks and make bold moves to stay ahead of the competition.

In order to embrace change and adaptability, it is important to foster a culture of innovation within your organization. Encourage your team members to think creatively and challenge the status quo. Create an environment where new ideas are welcomed and experimentation is encouraged. Provide opportunities for professional development and continuous learning, so that your team members can stay updated with the latest industry trends and technologies.

In conclusion, embracing change and adaptability is crucial for the success of any entrepreneur. It requires a growth mindset, a proactive approach, and a willingness to take risks. By embracing change, entrepreneurs can stay ahead of the curve, seize new opportunities, and build a thriving business in an ever-changing world.

Section 1.5
Setting Clear Goals and Vision

Setting clear goals and having a clear vision are essential components of the mindset of successful entrepreneurs. Without a clear direction and purpose, it becomes difficult to make strategic decisions and navigate the challenges that come with building a thriving business.

When setting goals, it is important to be specific and measurable. Vague goals such as "increase sales"or "expand the business"are not helpful in providing a clear roadmap for success. Instead, goals should be specific, such as "increase sales by 20% in the next quarter"or "expand into three new markets within the next year."By setting specific goals, entrepreneurs can track their progress and make adjustments as needed.

In addition to being specific, goals should also be measurable. This means that there should be a way to track and quantify progress towards the goal. For example, if the goal is to increase customer satisfaction, entrepreneurs can measure this by conducting customer surveys or tracking customer feedback. Measurable goals provide a sense of accountability and allow entrepreneurs to assess whether they are on track or need to make changes to their strategies.

Having a clear vision is equally important as setting clear goals. A vision is a long-term aspiration or desired outcome for the business. It provides a sense of purpose and direction, guiding the decisions and actions of the entrepreneur. A clear vision helps entrepreneurs stay focused and motivated, even in the face of challenges and setbacks.

To develop a clear vision, entrepreneurs should ask themselves questions such as "What do I want my business to achieve in the next five years?"or "What impact do I want my business to have on the world?"By answering these questions, entrepreneurs can articulate their vision and use it as a guiding principle for their business.

Setting clear goals and having a clear vision go hand in hand. Goals provide the actionable steps towards achieving the vision, while the vision provides the overarching purpose and direction for the goals. Together, they create a roadmap for success and help entrepreneurs stay focused and motivated.

It is important for entrepreneurs to regularly review and

reassess their goals and vision. As the business evolves and circumstances change, goals may need to be adjusted or new goals may need to be set. Similarly, the vision may need to be refined or updated to align with the changing landscape. By regularly reviewing and updating goals and vision, entrepreneurs can ensure that they are always working towards the most relevant and impactful objectives.

In conclusion, setting clear goals and having a clear vision are crucial elements of the mindset of successful entrepreneurs. Clear goals provide a roadmap for success, while a clear vision provides purpose and direction. By setting specific and measurable goals and articulating a clear vision, entrepreneurs can stay focused, motivated, and on track towards building a thriving business.

Section 1.6
Building Confidence and Self-Belief

Building confidence and self-belief is crucial for the success of any entrepreneur. Without a strong belief in oneself and the ability to overcome challenges, it can be difficult to navigate the ups and downs of building a thriving business. In this section, we will explore strategies and techniques that can help entrepreneurs build and maintain confidence in themselves and their abilities.

One of the first steps in building confidence is to recognize and acknowledge one's strengths and accomplishments. Take the time to reflect on past successes, no matter how small they may seem. Celebrate milestones and achievements, as they serve as reminders of what you are capable of. By focusing on your strengths and past successes, you can boost your confidence and belief in your abilities.

Another important aspect of building confidence is to surround yourself with a supportive network. Seek out mentors, advisors, and like-minded individuals who can provide guidance and encouragement. Surrounding yourself with positive and supportive people can help you stay motivated and inspired, especially during challenging times. Additionally, having a network of individuals who believe in you can help reinforce your own self-belief.

Taking calculated risks is another way to build confidence. Stepping outside of your comfort zone and embracing new challenges can be intimidating, but it is through these experiences that you can grow and develop as an entrepreneur. By pushing yourself to take risks and face your fears, you will not only build confidence but also gain valuable skills and knowledge that can contribute to your success.

It is also important to practice self-care and prioritize your well-being. Building confidence requires a strong foundation, and that starts with taking care of yourself physically, mentally, and emotionally. Make time for activities that bring you joy and help you relax. Engage in regular exercise, eat a balanced diet, and get enough sleep. Taking care of yourself will not only improve your overall well-being but also boost your confidence and ability to handle challenges.

Lastly, remember that building confidence is an ongoing

process. It is normal to have moments of self-doubt and uncertainty, but it is important to not let these moments define you. Instead, view them as opportunities for growth and learning. Embrace failure as a stepping stone to success and use setbacks as motivation to keep pushing forward. With perseverance and a belief in yourself, you can continue to build confidence and achieve your entrepreneurial goals.

In conclusion, building confidence and self-belief is essential for the success of any entrepreneur. By recognizing your strengths, surrounding yourself with a supportive network, taking calculated risks, practicing self-care, and embracing failure as a learning opportunity, you can cultivate the confidence needed to navigate the challenges of entrepreneurship. Remember, confidence is not something that happens overnight, but rather a continuous journey of self-discovery and growth.

Chapter 2

Identifying Profitable Business Opportunities

Section 2.1
Market Research and Analysis

Market research and analysis is a crucial step in identifying profitable business opportunities. It involves gathering and analyzing data about the market, industry trends, customer preferences, and competitors. By conducting thorough market research, entrepreneurs can gain valuable insights that will help them make informed decisions and develop effective strategies.

One of the first steps in market research is to define the target market. This involves identifying the specific group of customers who are most likely to be interested in the products or services offered by the business. By understanding the needs, preferences, and behaviors of the target market, entrepreneurs can tailor their offerings to meet their customers' demands.

Once the target market is defined, entrepreneurs can then gather data about the market size and potential demand. This can be done through surveys, interviews, focus groups, and analyzing existing market data. By understanding the size of the market and the potential demand for their products or services, entrepreneurs can assess the viability of their business idea and determine if there is enough market opportunity to support their venture.

Competitor analysis is another important aspect of market research. By studying the strengths and weaknesses of competitors, entrepreneurs can identify gaps in the market that they can exploit. This involves analyzing competitors' products, pricing strategies, marketing tactics, and customer feedback. By understanding what competitors are doing well and where they are falling short, entrepreneurs can position their business to offer unique value and stand out from the competition.

Market research also involves analyzing industry trends and identifying potential opportunities for innovation. By staying up-to-date with the latest trends and developments in the industry, entrepreneurs can identify emerging markets, new customer needs, and technological advancements that can be leveraged to create profitable business opportunities. This may involve attending industry conferences, reading industry publications, and networking with industry experts.

In addition to gathering data, entrepreneurs must also analyze and interpret the information collected during market research. This involves identifying patterns, trends, and insights that can inform business decisions. By analyzing the data, entrepreneurs can identify market gaps, customer pain points, and areas of opportunity that can be capitalized on.

Overall, market research and analysis is a critical step in identifying profitable business opportunities. By understanding the target market, assessing market demand, analyzing competitors, and staying informed about industry trends, entrepreneurs can make informed decisions and develop strategies that will set them up for success.

Section 2.2
Identifying Target Customers

Identifying target customers is a crucial step in building a successful business. Understanding who your customers are and what they want is essential for developing products or services that meet their needs and preferences. By identifying your target customers, you can tailor your marketing efforts and strategies to effectively reach and engage with them.

To identify your target customers, you need to conduct thorough market research and analysis. This involves gathering data and information about your potential customers, such as their demographics, psychographics, and buying behaviors. Demographics include factors like age, gender, income level, and location, while psychographics delve into their interests, values, and lifestyle choices. By analyzing this data, you can create customer profiles or buyer persona's that represent your ideal customers.

Once you have a clear understanding of your target customers, you can then assess the market demand for your products or services. This involves evaluating the size of the market, the level of competition, and any existing gaps or opportunities. By identifying the specific needs and pain points of your target customers, you can develop unique value propositions that differentiate your business from competitors.

Analyzing your competitors is another important aspect of identifying target customers. By studying your competitors' offerings, marketing strategies, and customer base, you can gain insights into their target customers and identify any untapped segments or niches. This information can help you refine your own target customer profiles and develop strategies to attract and retain customers.

Spotting trends and innovations in your industry is also crucial for identifying target customers. By staying up-to-date with the latest market trends, technological advancements, and consumer preferences, you can anticipate changes in customer behavior and adapt your business accordingly. This can involve incorporating new technologies, offering innovative products or services, or targeting emerging customer segments.

Evaluating potential risks is an important consideration when identifying target customers. It's essential to assess any potential challenges or obstacles that may arise in reaching and serving your target customers. This can include factors such as market saturation, changing regulations, or economic downturns. By identifying and addressing these risks early on, you can develop strategies to mitigate them and ensure the long-term success of your business.

In conclusion, identifying target customers is a critical step in identifying profitable business opportunities. By conducting thorough market research, analyzing customer data, and assessing market demand, you can develop a clear understanding of who your target customers are and what they want. This knowledge allows you to tailor your marketing efforts, develop unique value propositions, and effectively reach and engage with your target customers. By continuously monitoring market trends and evaluating potential risks, you can adapt your business strategies to stay ahead of the competition and ensure long-term success.

Section 2.3
Assessing Market Demand

Assessing market demand is a crucial step in identifying

profitable business opportunities. It involves understanding the needs and preferences of potential customers and determining whether there is sufficient demand for your product or service in the market.

To assess market demand, you need to conduct thorough market research. This includes gathering data on consumer behavior, market trends, and competitor analysis. By analyzing this information, you can gain insights into the size of the target market, the purchasing power of customers, and the level of competition you may face.

One effective way to assess market demand is by conducting surveys or interviews with potential customers. This allows you to gather direct feedback and understand their preferences, pain points, and willingness to pay for your product or service. By asking the right questions, you can uncover valuable insights that can help you refine your business idea and tailor your offering to meet customer needs.

Another important aspect of assessing market demand is analyzing market trends. This involves monitoring industry developments, technological advancements, and changes in consumer behavior. By staying informed about the latest trends, you can identify emerging opportunities and adapt your business strategy accordingly.

Competitor analysis is also crucial in assessing market demand. By studying your competitors, you can gain insights into their strengths, weaknesses, and market positioning. This information can help you identify gaps in the market that you can capitalize on, as well as potential threats and challenges you may face.

In addition to gathering data and conducting analysis, it is important to consider external factors that may impact market demand. Economic conditions, regulatory changes, and social trends can all influence consumer behavior and demand for certain products or services. By staying aware of these external factors, you can make informed decisions and adjust your business strategy accordingly.

Overall, assessing market demand is a critical step in identifying profitable business opportunities. By conducting thorough market research, analyzing consumer behavior, and staying informed about industry trends, you can gain valuable insights that can guide your business decisions and increase your chances of success.

Section 2.4
Analyzing Competitors

Analyzing competitors is a crucial step in identifying profitable business opportunities. By understanding the strengths and weaknesses of your competitors, you can gain valuable insights into the market landscape and position your business for success.

To begin the analysis, it is important to identify who your direct competitors are. These are the businesses that offer similar products or services to your target customers. Conduct thorough research to create a comprehensive list of competitors, including both established players and emerging startups.

Once you have identified your competitors, it is time to delve deeper into their strategies and operations. Start by examining their products or services. What unique features or benefits do they offer? How do their prices compare to yours? Understanding these factors will help you identify areas where you can differentiate your business and create a competitive advantage.

Next, analyze your competitors' marketing and branding strategies. How do they position themselves in the market? What channels do they use to reach their target customers? By studying their marketing efforts, you can gain insights into effective strategies and identify gaps that you can capitalize on.

Another important aspect to consider is your competitors' customer base. Who are their target customers? What demographics do they cater to? Understanding their customer profiles can help you identify untapped market segments or niche markets that you can target.

In addition to understanding your competitors' products, marketing strategies, and customer base, it is also crucial to assess their strengths and weaknesses. What are their core competencies? What areas do they excel in? By identifying their strengths, you can learn from their successes and find ways to improve your own business. Similarly, identifying their weaknesses can help you identify opportunities to outperform them in those areas.

Furthermore, keep an eye on your competitors' online presence and social media activities. What platforms do they use? How do they engage with their customers? Monitoring their online activities can provide valuable insights into their customer interactions and help you identify potential gaps in their customer service or engagement.

Lastly, it is important to stay updated on your competitors' latest developments and innovations. Are they launching new products or services? Are they expanding into new markets? By staying informed, you can anticipate market trends and proactively adapt your business strategies to stay ahead of the competition.

In conclusion, analyzing competitors is a critical step in identifying profitable business opportunities. By understanding your competitors' products, marketing strategies, customer base, strengths, weaknesses, online presence, and latest developments, you can gain valuable insights that will inform your own business strategies and help you position your business for success in the market.

Section 2.5
Spotting Trends and Innovations

In today's fast-paced and ever-changing business

landscape, staying ahead of the curve is crucial for entrepreneurs looking to identify profitable business opportunities. One effective way to do this is by spotting trends and innovations that have the potential to disrupt industries and create new markets.

Spotting trends involves observing patterns and shifts in consumer behavior, market dynamics, and technological advancements. By keeping a close eye on these trends, entrepreneurs can identify emerging opportunities and position themselves to capitalize on them.

One key aspect of spotting trends is understanding consumer preferences and demands. This involves conducting market research and analysis to identify emerging needs and desires. By staying attuned to changing consumer preferences, entrepreneurs can develop products or services that cater to these evolving demands.

Technological advancements also play a significant role in identifying trends and innovations. Entrepreneurs need to stay updated on the latest technological developments and assess how they can be leveraged to create new business opportunities. This could involve adopting new technologies, such as artificial intelligence or block chain, to streamline processes or create innovative solutions.

Another important aspect of spotting trends is keeping an eye on industry disruptor and innovators. By studying successful startups and industry leaders, entrepreneurs can gain insights into emerging business models, products, or services that have the potential to reshape industries. This could involve attending industry conferences, networking with industry experts, or following thought leaders in the field.

In addition to external factors, entrepreneurs should also pay attention to internal factors within their own organizations. By fostering a culture of innovation and encouraging employees to think creatively, entrepreneurs can tap into the collective intelligence of their teams to identify new trends and opportunities. This could involve setting up brainstorming sessions, creating innovation challenges, or providing resources for continuous learning and development.

Spotting trends and innovations is not a one-time activity but an ongoing process. Entrepreneurs need to continuously monitor the market, consumer behavior, and technological advancements to stay ahead of the competition. By staying proactive and adaptable, entrepreneurs can position themselves to seize new opportunities and build a thriving business.

In the next section, we will explore the importance of evaluating potential risks when identifying profitable business opportunities. By understanding and mitigating risks, entrepreneurs can make informed decisions and increase their chances of success.

Section 2.6
Evaluating Potential Risks

When identifying profitable business opportunities, it is crucial to also consider the potential risks associated with each opportunity. Evaluating potential risks allows entrepreneurs to make informed decisions and develop strategies to mitigate or manage these risks effectively.

One of the first steps in evaluating potential risks is conducting a thorough risk assessment. This involves identifying and analyzing the various risks that could impact the success of the business opportunity. These risks can include market volatility, competition, regulatory changes, economic downturns, and technological advancements, among others.

Market volatility is a common risk that entrepreneurs need to consider. Fluctuations in the market can affect consumer demand, pricing, and overall profitability. By analyzing market trends and historical data, entrepreneurs can gain insights into potential market risks and develop contingency plans to minimize their impact.

Competition is another significant risk that entrepreneurs must evaluate. Understanding the competitive landscape and analyzing competitors' strengths and weaknesses can help entrepreneurs identify potential threats and develop strategies to differentiate their business and gain a competitive advantage.

Regulatory changes can also pose risks to a business

opportunity. Entrepreneurs need to stay updated on relevant laws and regulations that may impact their industry or target market. By proactively monitoring and adapting to regulatory changes, entrepreneurs can minimize legal and compliance risks.

Economic downturns can significantly impact the success of a business opportunity. During economic downturns, consumer spending tends to decrease, and businesses may face challenges in generating revenue. Evaluating the potential impact of economic downturns and developing strategies to diversify revenue streams or target more resilient markets can help mitigate this risk.

Technological advancements can both present opportunities and risks. While embracing technology can enhance efficiency and competitiveness, entrepreneurs need to evaluate the potential risks associated with technological disruptions. This includes assessing the impact of emerging technologies on the business model and ensuring the business is adaptable to technological changes.

Once potential risks have been identified, entrepreneurs should develop risk management strategies. This involves implementing measures to mitigate or minimize the impact of risks and developing contingency plans to address potential challenges. Risk management strategies may include diversifying revenue streams, establishing strong relationships with suppliers and partners, implementing robust cyber security measures, and maintaining adequate insurance coverage.

Regular monitoring and reassessment of potential risks are essential to ensure the continued success of the business opportunity. As the business landscape evolves, new risks may emerge, and existing risks may change in severity. By staying vigilant and adapting risk management strategies accordingly, entrepreneurs can navigate potential risks and increase the likelihood of building a profitable and sustainable business.

In conclusion, evaluating potential risks is a critical step in identifying profitable business opportunities. By conducting a thorough risk assessment, entrepreneurs can gain a comprehensive understanding of the risks associated with a particular opportunity. Developing risk management strategies and regularly monitoring and reassessing potential risks are essential for mitigating the impact of these risks and increasing the chances of building a thriving and successful business.

Chapter 3
Creating a Solid Business Plan

Section 3.1
Defining Your Business Model

Defining your business model is a crucial step in creating a solid business plan. It serves as the foundation for your entire business strategy and determines how you will generate revenue, deliver value to customers, and sustain profitability.

A business model outlines the key elements of your business, including your target market, value proposition, revenue streams, cost structure, and key activities. It provides a clear roadmap for how your business will operate and create value for customers.

To define your business model, start by identifying your target market. Who are your ideal customers? What are their needs, preferences, and pain points? Understanding your target market will help you tailor your products or services to meet their specific demands.

Next, determine your value proposition. What unique value do you offer to customers? How does your product or service solve their problems or fulfill their desires? Your value proposition should differentiate you from competitors and clearly communicate the benefits customers can expect.

Once you have identified your target market and value proposition, you can determine your revenue streams.

How will you generate income? Will you sell products, offer services, or utilize a subscription-based model? Consider different pricing strategies and revenue sources to maximize profitability.

Alongside revenue streams, you need to consider your cost structure. What are the key expenses associated with running your business? This includes costs such as production, marketing, distribution, and overhead. Understanding your costs will help you set pricing and ensure profitability.

In addition to revenue and costs, your business model should outline key activities required to deliver value to customers. This includes activities such as product development, marketing and sales, customer support, and operations. Identifying these key activities will help you allocate resources effectively and streamline your operations.

As you define your business model, it is important to consider potential risks and challenges. Assess the market and competitive landscape to identify potential threats and develop strategies to mitigate them. This could involve diversifying revenue streams, building strong relationships with suppliers, or implementing contingency plans.

Lastly, your business model should be flexible and adaptable. As your business evolves and market conditions change, you may need to adjust your model to stay competitive. Regularly review and refine your business model to ensure it remains aligned with your goals and market dynamics.

In conclusion, defining your business model is a critical step in creating a solid business plan. It provides a clear framework for how your business will operate, generate revenue, and deliver value to customers. By carefully considering your target market, value proposition, revenue streams, cost structure, and key activities, you can create a business model that sets you up for long-term success.

Section 3.2
Setting Realistic Financial Goals

Setting realistic financial goals is a crucial step in creating a solid business plan. Without clear and achievable financial goals, it becomes difficult to measure the success and progress of your business. In this section, we will discuss the importance of setting realistic financial goals and provide practical tips on how to do so effectively.

When setting financial goals, it is essential to consider both short-term and long-term objectives. Short-term goals focus on immediate financial needs, such as covering expenses and generating enough revenue to sustain the business. Long-term goals, on the other hand, involve planning for future growth and profitability. To set realistic financial goals, start by conducting a thorough analysis of your business's current financial situation. This includes assessing your revenue streams, expenses, and cash flow. By understanding your financial position, you can identify areas for improvement and set goals that align with your business's capabilities.

When setting financial goals, it is crucial to be specific and measurable. Instead of simply aiming to increase revenue, set a specific target, such as increasing revenue by 10% within the next quarter. This allows you to track your progress and make adjustments if necessary.

Additionally, it is important to consider external factors that may impact your financial goals. This includes market conditions, industry trends, and potential risks. By taking these factors into account, you can set more realistic and achievable goals that are in line with the current business environment.

Another key aspect of setting realistic financial goals is ensuring they are attainable. While it is important to aim high, setting goals that are too ambitious can lead to frustration and disappointment. Consider your business's resources, capabilities, and limitations when setting financial goals to ensure they are within reach.

Furthermore, it is essential to set a timeline for achieving your financial goals. This provides a sense of urgency and helps you stay focused and motivated. Break down your goals into smaller milestones and set deadlines for each milestone. This allows you to track your progress and make adjustments if necessary.

In addition to setting financial goals, it is important to regularly review and reassess them. As your business evolves and market conditions change, your financial goals may need to be adjusted. Regularly monitoring your progress and making necessary adjustments ensures that your goals remain relevant and achievable.

In conclusion, setting realistic financial goals is a critical component of creating a solid business plan. By considering your business's current financial situation, being specific and measurable, considering external factors, ensuring attainability, setting a timeline, and regularly reviewing and reassessing your goals, you can set realistic financial goals that drive the success and growth of your business.

Section 3.3
Developing a Marketing Strategy

Developing a marketing strategy is a crucial step in creating a solid business plan. A well-defined marketing strategy helps entrepreneurs effectively promote their products or services, reach their target audience, and ultimately drive sales and revenue. In this section, we will explore the key components of developing a marketing strategy and provide practical tips for success.

First and foremost, it is essential to clearly define your target market. Understanding your ideal customers' demographics, preferences, and needs will enable you to tailor your marketing efforts to effectively reach and engage them. Conducting market research and analysis can provide valuable insights into your target market's behavior, preferences, and purchasing habits.

Once you have identified your target market, it is crucial to establish your unique selling proposition (USP). Your USP is what sets your business apart from competitors and highlights the value you offer to customers. It could be a unique feature, exceptional customer service, or a competitive pricing strategy. Clearly articulating your USP will help you differentiate your business and attract customers.

Next, you need to determine the most effective marketing channels to reach your target audience. This could include traditional channels such as print advertising, television, or radio, as well as digital channels like social media, email marketing, and search engine optimization (SEO). Understanding where your target audience spends their time and how they prefer to receive information will help you allocate your marketing budget effectively.

In addition to selecting the right marketing channels, it is crucial to develop compelling and engaging content that resonates with your target audience. Your content should communicate your brand's values, showcase your products or services, and provide valuable information or entertainment to your audience. Creating a content calendar and consistently delivering high-quality content will help build brand awareness and establish your business as a trusted authority in your industry.

Another important aspect of developing a marketing strategy is setting clear and measurable goals. Whether it's increasing brand awareness, generating leads, or driving sales, your marketing goals should be specific, measurable, attainable, relevant, and time-bound (SMART). Regularly tracking and analyzing your marketing efforts' performance will allow you to make data-driven decisions and optimize your strategy for better results.

Furthermore, it is crucial to allocate your marketing budget effectively. Consider the return on investment (ROI) of each marketing channel and prioritize those that have proven to be most effective in reaching your target audience. It is also important to regularly review and adjust your marketing budget based on the performance of different channels and campaigns.

Lastly, remember that a marketing strategy is not a one-time effort but an ongoing process. The market and consumer preferences are constantly evolving, so it is essential to stay updated with the latest trends and adapt your strategy accordingly. Regularly monitor your competitors' marketing activities and industry trends to identify new opportunities and stay ahead of the curve.

In conclusion, developing a marketing strategy is a critical component of creating a solid business plan. By understanding your target market, defining your unique selling proposition, selecting the right marketing channels, creating compelling content, setting clear goals, allocating your budget effectively, and staying adaptable, you can build a successful marketing strategy that drives business growth and success.

Section 3.4
Establishing Operational Processes

Establishing operational processes is a crucial step in

creating a solid business plan. These processes are the backbone of your business and ensure that your day-to-day operations run smoothly and efficiently. By establishing clear and effective operational processes, you can streamline your business operations, reduce costs, and improve overall productivity.

One of the first steps in establishing operational processes is to identify and document all the key activities and tasks that need to be performed within your business. This includes everything from production and inventory management to customer service and order fulfillment. By mapping out these processes, you can gain a clear understanding of how your business operates and identify any areas that may need improvement.

Once you have identified the key processes, it is important to define clear roles and responsibilities for each task. This ensures that everyone in your organization knows what is expected of them and can work together seamlessly. Clearly defining roles also helps to avoid confusion and duplication of efforts, leading to increased efficiency and productivity.

In addition to defining roles, it is important to establish standard operating procedures (SOPs) for each process.

SOPs outline the step-by-step instructions for carrying out specific tasks and ensure consistency and quality in your operations. These procedures should be documented and easily accessible to all employees, providing them with a reference guide to follow.

Another important aspect of establishing operational processes is implementing effective communication channels. Clear and open communication is essential for smooth operations and collaboration within your team. This can be achieved through regular team meetings, email updates, and the use of project management tools that facilitate communication and collaboration.

Furthermore, it is crucial to regularly review and evaluate your operational processes to identify areas for improvement. This can be done through performance metrics, customer feedback, and employee suggestions. By continuously monitoring and analyzing your processes, you can identify bottlenecks, inefficiencies, and opportunities for optimization.

Automation and technology can also play a significant role in establishing operational processes. By leveraging technology, you can automate repetitive tasks, streamline workflow, and improve overall efficiency.

This can free up valuable time and resources, allowing you to focus on more strategic aspects of your business. Lastly, it is important to ensure that your operational processes are flexible and adaptable to changing circumstances. As your business grows and evolves, your processes may need to be adjusted to accommodate new challenges and opportunities. By regularly reviewing and updating your processes, you can ensure that your business remains agile and responsive to market changes.

In conclusion, establishing operational processes is a critical component of creating a solid business plan. By mapping out key activities, defining roles and responsibilities, implementing SOPs, fostering effective communication, and leveraging technology, you can streamline your operations and drive business success. Regularly reviewing and adapting your processes ensures that your business remains efficient, productive, and adaptable in an ever-changing business landscape.

Section 3.5
Building a Strong Team

Building a strong team is crucial for the success of any business. A strong team not only brings together diverse skills and expertise but also fosters a positive work environment and promotes collaboration. In this section, we will explore the key steps to building a strong team that will support your business goals and help you achieve long-term success.

First and foremost, it is important to clearly define the roles and responsibilities within your team. Each team member should have a clear understanding of their role and how it contributes to the overall success of the business. This clarity will not only prevent confusion but also ensure that everyone is working towards a common goal.

When building your team, it is essential to hire individuals who not only possess the necessary skills and qualifications but also align with your company's values and culture. Look for candidates who are not only competent but also share your passion and vision for the business. This alignment will foster a sense of belonging and commitment among team members.

Effective communication is another key aspect of building a strong team. Encourage open and transparent communication among team members, and establish regular channels for feedback and discussion. This will not only promote collaboration but also help identify and address any issues or challenges that may arise.

In addition to hiring the right individuals, it is important to invest in their development and growth. Provide opportunities for training and professional development, and encourage continuous learning within your team. This will not only enhance their skills and knowledge but also demonstrate your commitment to their personal and professional growth.

Building a strong team also involves fostering a positive work environment. Encourage a culture of respect, trust, and collaboration among team members. Recognize and appreciate their contributions, and create opportunities for team-building activities and social interactions. A positive work environment will not only boost morale but also improve productivity and overall team performance.

Lastly, as a leader, it is important to delegate responsibilities and empower your team members. Trust them to make decisions and take ownership of their work. This not only builds their confidence but also allows you to focus on strategic aspects of the business.

Effective delegation and empowerment will not only enhance team performance but also create a sense of ownership and accountability among team members.

In conclusion, building a strong team is essential for the success of your business. By clearly defining roles and responsibilities, hiring the right individuals, fostering effective communication, investing in development, creating a positive work environment, and delegating responsibilities, you can build a team that will support your business goals and contribute to long-term success. Remember, a strong team is the foundation of a thriving business.

Section 3.6
Securing Funding and Resources

Securing funding and resources is a crucial aspect of creating a solid business plan. Without adequate financial support and necessary resources, it can be challenging to turn your business idea into a reality. In this section, we will explore various strategies and approaches to help you secure the funding and resources needed to launch and grow your business.

One of the first steps in securing funding is to clearly define your financial needs. This involves determining how much capital you require to start and operate your business, as well as identifying any additional resources or assets that may be necessary. By having a clear understanding of your financial needs, you can effectively communicate your requirements to potential investors or lenders.

When seeking funding, it is important to explore a variety of options. Traditional sources of funding include banks, venture capitalists, and angel investors. However, there are also alternative options such as crowd funding platforms and government grants that may be worth considering. Each funding source has its own requirements and criteria, so it is essential to research and understand the specific terms and conditions associated with each option.

To increase your chances of securing funding, it is crucial to develop a compelling business plan. Your business plan should outline your company's mission, vision, and goals, as well as provide a detailed analysis of your target market, competitors, and financial projections. A well-crafted business plan demonstrates your understanding of the market and your ability to generate revenue, which can instill confidence in potential investors or lenders.

Networking and building relationships with potential investors or lenders can also be instrumental in securing funding. Attending industry events, joining entrepreneurial communities, and participating in pitch competitions can provide valuable opportunities to connect with individuals who may be interested in supporting your business. Building trust and rapport with potential investors or lenders is essential, as they are more likely to invest in businesses they believe in and have a personal connection with.

In addition to securing financial resources, it is important to consider other necessary resources for your business. This may include physical assets such as office space, equipment, or inventory, as well as intangible resources such as intellectual property or technology. Assessing your resource needs and developing a plan to acquire or leverage these resources is essential for the successful implementation of your business plan.

Lastly, it is important to remember that securing funding

and resources is an ongoing process. As your business grows and evolves, your financial and resource needs may change. Continuously evaluating and reassessing your funding and resource requirements will ensure that you have the necessary support to sustain and expand your business.

In conclusion, securing funding and resources is a critical component of creating a solid business plan. By clearly defining your financial needs, exploring various funding options, developing a compelling business plan, networking with potential investors or lenders, and assessing your resource requirements, you can increase your chances of securing the necessary support to turn your business idea into a thriving reality. Remember, securing funding and resources is an ongoing process, so it is important to continuously evaluate and adapt your approach as your business grows and evolves.

Section 3.7
Legal and Regulatory Considerations

When creating a solid business plan, it is crucial to

consider the legal and regulatory aspects that may impact your business operations. Failing to comply with applicable laws and regulations can result in severe consequences, including fines, legal disputes, and damage to your reputation. Therefore, it is essential to thoroughly understand and address these considerations in your business plan.

One of the first steps in addressing legal and regulatory considerations is to identify the specific laws and regulations that apply to your industry and business activities. This may include industry-specific regulations, such as health and safety standards, environmental regulations, licensing requirements, and intellectual property laws. It is important to conduct thorough research and consult with legal professionals to ensure you have a comprehensive understanding of the legal landscape.

Once you have identified the relevant laws and regulations, you need to outline how your business will comply with them. This may involve implementing specific policies and procedures, obtaining necessary licenses and permits, and ensuring your business operations align with the requirements set forth by regulatory bodies. It is crucial to allocate resources and budget for legal compliance to avoid any potential legal issues down the line.

In addition to compliance, it is important to consider any potential legal risks and liabilities that your business may face. This includes understanding contractual obligations, potential disputes with customers or suppliers, and the protection of your intellectual property. By addressing these risks in your business plan, you can demonstrate to potential investors and stakeholders that you have considered and mitigated potential legal challenges.

Furthermore, it is essential to stay updated on any changes in laws and regulations that may impact your business. Regulatory environments are constantly evolving, and it is crucial to adapt your business practices accordingly. This may involve regularly reviewing and updating your policies and procedures, seeking legal advice when necessary, and staying informed about industry-specific developments.

Lastly, it is important to consider the potential impact of international laws and regulations if you plan to expand your business globally. Different countries have varying legal frameworks, and it is crucial to understand and comply with the laws of each jurisdiction you operate in.

This may involve consulting with legal experts who specialize in international business law and ensuring your business practices align with local regulations.

In conclusion, legal and regulatory considerations are an integral part of creating a solid business plan. By thoroughly understanding and addressing these considerations, you can ensure legal compliance, mitigate potential risks, and demonstrate to stakeholders that your business is committed to operating ethically and responsibly. It is crucial to allocate resources for legal compliance, stay updated on changes in laws and regulations, and seek legal advice when necessary to navigate the complex legal landscape successfully.

Section 3.8 Measuring and Tracking Progress

Measuring and tracking progress is a crucial aspect of creating a solid business plan. Without proper measurement and tracking, it becomes difficult to assess the effectiveness of your strategies and make informed decisions for the future of your business.

One of the key metrics to consider when measuring progress is financial performance. This includes tracking revenue, expenses, and profitability. By regularly monitoring these financial indicators, you can identify areas of improvement and take necessary actions to optimize your business operations.

In addition to financial metrics, it is important to track key performance indicators (KPIs) that are specific to your industry and business goals. These KPIs can vary depending on the nature of your business, but some common examples include customer acquisition rate, customer retention rate, conversion rate, and average order value. By setting targets for these KPIs and regularly monitoring them, you can gauge the effectiveness of your marketing and sales efforts and make adjustments as needed.

Another important aspect of measuring and tracking progress is setting milestones and benchmarks. These can be short-term or long-term goals that serve as checkpoints for evaluating your progress. By breaking down your business plan into smaller milestones, you can track your progress more effectively and stay motivated as you achieve each milestone.

To measure and track progress, it is essential to establish a system for data collection and analysis. This can involve implementing software or tools that automate data collection and provide real-time insights. By regularly reviewing and analyzing the data, you can identify trends, patterns, and areas for improvement.

Communication and reporting are also crucial when it comes to measuring and tracking progress. Regularly sharing updates and reports with key stakeholders, such as investors, employees, and partners, helps keep everyone informed and aligned with the business goals. It also provides an opportunity for feedback and collaboration, which can further enhance the effectiveness of your business plan.

Lastly, it is important to remember that measuring and tracking progress is an ongoing process. As your business evolves and market conditions change, it is necessary to adapt your metrics and tracking methods accordingly. By continuously monitoring and evaluating your progress, you can make data-driven decisions and ensure the long-term success of your business.

In conclusion, measuring and tracking progress is a critical component of creating a solid business plan. By monitoring financial performance, tracking key performance indicators, setting milestones, implementing data collection and analysis systems, and maintaining effective communication, you can assess the effectiveness of your strategies and make informed decisions for the future of your business.

Chapter 4
Effective Marketing and Branding Strategies

Section 4.1
Building a Strong Brand Identity

Building a strong brand identity is crucial for the success of any business. A brand identity is more than just a logo or a tagline; it encompasses the overall perception and image that customers have of your company. It is what sets you apart from your competitors and creates a lasting impression in the minds of your target audience.

To build a strong brand identity, you need to start by clearly defining your brand's values, mission, and vision. What do you stand for as a company? What are your core beliefs and principles? These elements will serve as the foundation for your brand identity and will guide all your branding efforts.

Once you have defined your brand's values, it's important to consistently communicate them across all your marketing channels. This includes your website, social media profiles, advertising campaigns, and even your packaging. Consistency is key in building a strong brand identity, as it helps to create a sense of familiarity and trust with your audience.

Another important aspect of building a strong brand identity is understanding your target audience. Who are your ideal customers? What are their needs, desires, and pain points? By understanding your target audience, you can tailor your brand messaging and visuals to resonate with them on a deeper level. This will help you build a strong emotional connection with your customers, which is essential for brand loyalty.

Visual elements such as your logo, color palette, and typography also play a crucial role in building a strong brand identity. These elements should be carefully chosen to reflect your brand's personality and values. For example, if your brand is known for being innovative and cutting-edge, you may opt for a modern and bold logo design. On the other hand, if your brand is focused on sustainability and eco-friendliness, you may choose earthy tones and organic shapes.

Consistency in your visual branding is equally important. Your logo, color palette, and typography should be used consistently across all your marketing materials to create a cohesive and recognizable brand identity. This consistency helps to build brand recognition and makes it easier for customers to identify and remember your brand.

In addition to visual elements, your brand's tone of voice and messaging also contribute to its identity. How do you communicate with your audience? Is your brand voice formal and professional, or casual and friendly? Your tone of voice should align with your brand's values and resonate with your target audience. Consistency in your messaging is also important, as it helps to reinforce your brand's identity and build trust with your customers.

Building a strong brand identity takes time and effort, but the benefits are well worth it. A strong brand identity helps to differentiate your business from competitors, build trust and loyalty with customers, and ultimately drive business growth. By clearly defining your brand's values, consistently communicating them, understanding your target audience, and carefully crafting your visual and verbal branding, you can create a strong and memorable brand identity that sets you apart in the marketplace.

Section 4.2
Targeted Marketing Campaigns

Targeted marketing campaigns are a crucial aspect of any successful business's marketing strategy. These campaigns involve tailoring your marketing efforts to reach a specific audience or target market, rather than taking a one-size-fits-all approach. By focusing your marketing efforts on a specific group of people who are most likely to be interested in your products or services, you can maximize your return on investment and increase the effectiveness of your marketing efforts.

One of the first steps in creating a targeted marketing campaign is identifying your target audience. This involves conducting market research to understand the demographics, interests, and behaviors of your potential customers. By gaining a deep understanding of your target audience, you can create marketing messages and content that resonate with them and address their specific needs and pain points.

Once you have identified your target audience, you can then develop a marketing strategy that is tailored to reach and engage with them. This may involve using different marketing channels and tactics that are most effective in reaching your target audience. For example, if your target audience is primarily active on social media, you may focus your marketing efforts on platforms like Facebook, Instagram, or LinkedIn.

In addition to selecting the right marketing channels, it is important to create compelling and relevant content that speaks directly to your target audience. This can include creating personalized messages, using language and imagery that resonates with your audience, and addressing their specific pain points and desires. By creating content that is tailored to your target audience, you can capture their attention and increase the likelihood of them taking action, such as making a purchase or signing up for your services.

Another important aspect of targeted marketing campaigns is tracking and measuring their effectiveness. By using analytics and tracking tools, you can monitor the performance of your campaigns and make data-driven decisions to optimize your marketing efforts. This may involve analyzing metrics such as click-through rates, conversion rates, and customer engagement to understand what is working and what needs improvement. By continuously monitoring and analyzing the results of your campaigns, you can make adjustments and improvements to ensure that your marketing efforts are delivering the desired results.

Overall, targeted marketing campaigns are a powerful tool for businesses to reach and engage with their ideal customers. By tailoring your marketing efforts to a specific audience, you can increase the effectiveness of your marketing efforts and maximize your return on investment. By understanding your target audience, selecting the right marketing channels, creating compelling content, and tracking the performance of your campaigns, you can create targeted marketing campaigns that drive results and contribute to the overall success of your business.

Section 4.3
Utilizing Social Media and Digital Marketing

In today's digital age, social media and digital marketing have become essential tools for entrepreneurs looking to promote their businesses and connect with their target audience. With billions of people using social media platforms like Facebook, Instagram, Twitter, and LinkedIn, harnessing the power of these platforms can significantly impact the success of your marketing efforts.

One of the key advantages of utilizing social media for marketing is its ability to reach a large and diverse audience. By creating engaging and shareable content, entrepreneurs can increase brand visibility and attract potential customers. Social media platforms also provide valuable insights and analytics that can help entrepreneurs understand their audience better and tailor their marketing strategies accordingly.

When it comes to digital marketing, entrepreneurs have a wide range of options to choose from. Search engine optimization (SEO) is a crucial aspect of digital marketing, as it helps businesses rank higher in search engine results and drive organic traffic to their websites. Pay-per-click (PPC) advertising allows entrepreneurs to target specific keywords and demographics, ensuring their ads are seen by the right audience.

Email marketing is another effective digital marketing strategy that allows entrepreneurs to nurture relationships with their customers and drive repeat business. By sending personalized and relevant emails, entrepreneurs can keep their audience engaged and informed about new products, promotions, and updates.

Social media and digital marketing also offer entrepreneurs the opportunity to engage with their audience in real-time. By responding to comments, messages, and reviews, entrepreneurs can build trust and credibility with their customers. Additionally, social media platforms provide a space for entrepreneurs to showcase their expertise and thought leadership through blog posts, videos, and live streams.

To effectively utilize social media and digital marketing, entrepreneurs should develop a comprehensive strategy that aligns with their overall marketing goals. This includes identifying the most relevant social media platforms for their target audience, creating a content calendar, and regularly monitoring and analyzing the performance of their campaigns.

In conclusion, social media and digital marketing have revolutionized the way entrepreneurs promote their businesses and connect with their audience. By utilizing these powerful tools, entrepreneurs can increase brand visibility, drive traffic to their websites, and engage with their customers in meaningful ways. With the right strategy and consistent effort, social media and digital marketing can play a significant role in the success of any business.

Section 4.4
Creating Compelling Content

Creating compelling content is a crucial aspect of effective marketing and branding strategies. In today's digital age, where consumers are constantly bombarded with information, it is essential to create content that stands out and captures their attention. Compelling content not only helps to attract and engage your target audience but also builds trust and credibility for your brand.

To create compelling content, it is important to understand your target audience and their needs. Conduct thorough market research to gain insights into their preferences, interests, and pain points. This will enable you to tailor your content to resonate with them and provide value.

One key element of compelling content is storytelling. Humans are naturally drawn to stories, and incorporating storytelling techniques into your content can make it more relatable and memorable. Use narratives, anecdotes, and real-life examples to connect with your audience on an emotional level and make your content more compelling.

Another important aspect of creating compelling content is providing valuable information and insights.

Your content should offer solutions to your audience's problems, answer their questions, or provide them with valuable knowledge. This will position your brand as an authority in your industry and build trust with your audience.

Visual elements also play a significant role in creating compelling content. Incorporate eye-catching images, videos, infographics, and other visual elements to make your content more engaging and shareable. Visual content is more likely to be remembered and shared by your audience, increasing your brand's visibility and reach.

In addition to visual elements, the format and structure of your content are also important. Break up your content into easily digestible sections with subheadings, bullet points, and numbered lists. This makes it easier for your audience to skim through and find the information they are looking for. Use a conversational tone and avoid jargon or technical language that may alienate your audience.

Furthermore, it is essential to optimize your content for search engines. Conduct keyword research to identify relevant keywords and incorporate them naturally into your content. This will improve your content's visibility in search engine results and attract organic traffic to your website.

Lastly, don't forget to promote your content through various channels. Share it on your social media platforms, email newsletters, and other relevant online communities. Encourage your audience to share and engage with your content, as this will increase its reach and impact.

In conclusion, creating compelling content is a vital component of effective marketing and branding strategies. By understanding your target audience, incorporating storytelling techniques, providing valuable information, using visual elements, optimizing for search engines, and promoting your content, you can create content that captivates your audience and drives results for your business.

Section 4.5
Building Customer Loyalty and Engagement

Building customer loyalty and engagement is crucial for the long-term success of any business. When customers feel a strong connection to a brand, they are more likely to become repeat customers and advocates for the company. In this section, we will explore strategies for building customer loyalty and engagement. One of the most effective ways to build customer loyalty is by providing exceptional customer service. When customers have a positive experience with a company, they are more likely to continue doing business with them. This includes responding promptly to customer inquiries, resolving issues in a timely manner, and going above and beyond to exceed customer expectations.

Another strategy for building customer loyalty is by creating a personalized experience for each customer. This can be done through targeted marketing campaigns, personalized emails, and tailored product recommendations. By understanding the unique needs and preferences of each customer, businesses can create a more meaningful and personalized experience, which can lead to increased loyalty and engagement.

In addition to providing exceptional customer service

and personalization, businesses can also build customer loyalty through loyalty programs and rewards. Offering incentives such as discounts, exclusive offers, and loyalty points can encourage customers to continue doing business with a company. These programs not only reward customers for their loyalty but also create a sense of exclusivity and belonging, which can further strengthen the customer's connection to the brand.

Furthermore, building customer loyalty and engagement requires ongoing communication and relationship-building. This can be achieved through regular email newsletters, social media engagement, and personalized follow-ups. By staying in touch with customers and keeping them informed about new products, promotions, and company updates, businesses can maintain a strong connection and encourage ongoing engagement.

Lastly, it is important to actively listen to customer feedback and incorporate it into business decisions. By soliciting feedback through surveys, reviews, and social media, businesses can gain valuable insights into customer preferences and areas for improvement. By addressing customer concerns and making necessary changes, businesses can demonstrate their commitment to customer satisfaction and build trust and loyalty.

In conclusion, building customer loyalty and engagement is essential for the success of any business. By providing exceptional customer service, personalizing the customer experience, offering loyalty programs and rewards, maintaining ongoing communication, and actively listening to customer feedback, businesses can create a strong and loyal customer base. This not only leads to increased customer retention and repeat business but also positive word-of-mouth referrals and brand advocacy.

Section 4.6
Leveraging Influencer Marketing

In today's digital age, influencer marketing has become a powerful tool for businesses to reach their target audience and build brand awareness. Influencer are individuals who have a significant following on social media platforms and can influence the purchasing decisions of their followers. Leveraging influencer marketing can help businesses tap into the trust and credibility that influencer have established with their audience.

One of the key benefits of influencer marketing is the ability to reach a highly targeted audience. By partnering with influences who align with your brand values and target market, you can ensure that your message reaches the right people. Influencer have already built a loyal following who trust their recommendations, making it easier for businesses to connect with potential customers.

When leveraging influencer marketing, it's important to choose influences whose audience aligns with your target market. This ensures that your message resonates with the right people and increases the likelihood of conversion. Conduct thorough research to identify influencer who have a genuine interest in your industry or niche, as well as a strong engagement rate with their audience.

Collaborating with influences can take various forms, such as sponsored posts, product reviews, or brand partnerships. It's essential to establish clear goals and expectations for the collaboration to ensure both parties are aligned. This includes defining the scope of the partnership, the deliverables, and any specific messaging or guidelines that need to be followed.

To maximize the impact of influencer marketing, businesses should focus on building authentic relationships with influences. This involves engaging with their content, sharing their posts, and genuinely supporting their work. By nurturing these relationships, businesses can establish long-term partnerships that benefit both parties.

In addition to reaching a wider audience, influencer marketing can also help businesses improve their brand perception. When an influencer endorses a product or service, it adds credibility and trust to the brand. This can lead to increased brand awareness, positive brand associations, and ultimately, higher customer loyalty.

However, it's important to note that influencer marketing is not a one-size-fits-all solution. Businesses should carefully evaluate the ROI of each influencer partnership and track the success of their campaigns. This can be done through tracking links, discount codes, or specific landing pages to measure the impact of influencer collaborations on sales and brand metrics.

In conclusion, leveraging influencer marketing can be a highly effective strategy for businesses to enhance their marketing and branding efforts. By partnering with influences who have a genuine connection with their audience, businesses can tap into their influence and reach a highly targeted market. However, it's crucial to approach influencer marketing with a strategic mindset, setting clear goals and expectations, and continuously evaluating the success of each collaboration.

Chapter 5
Sales and Customer Acquisition

Section 5.1
Developing a Sales Strategy

Developing a sales strategy is crucial for the success of any business. It involves creating a plan to effectively sell products or services to target customers and acquire new customers. A well-defined sales strategy helps businesses maximize their revenue and achieve their sales goals.

To develop a sales strategy, it is important to first understand your target customers. Who are they? What are their needs and pain points? By identifying your target customers, you can tailor your sales approach to meet their specific needs and preferences.

Once you have a clear understanding of your target customers, you can then determine the best sales channels to reach them. This could include direct sales, online sales, or partnerships with distributors or retailers. Each sales channel has its own advantages and disadvantages, so it is important to choose the ones that align with your business goals and target customers.

In addition to choosing the right sales channels, it is also important to define your sales process. This includes identifying the steps involved in the sales cycle, from prospecting and lead generation to closing the sale and follow-up. By mapping out the sales process, you can ensure that each step is executed effectively and efficiently.

Another key aspect of developing a sales strategy is setting sales targets and goals. This involves determining the desired sales volume, revenue, and market share. Setting realistic and achievable goals is important to keep your sales team motivated and focused. It also helps you track your progress and make necessary adjustments to your sales strategy.

Furthermore, a successful sales strategy involves

training and equipping your sales team with the necessary skills and tools. This includes providing product knowledge training, sales techniques, and effective communication skills. By investing in your sales team's development, you can enhance their performance and increase their chances of success.

Lastly, it is important to regularly evaluate and refine your sales strategy. This involves analyzing sales data, customer feedback, and market trends to identify areas for improvement. By continuously monitoring and adjusting your sales strategy, you can stay ahead of the competition and adapt to changing market conditions.

In conclusion, developing a sales strategy is essential for businesses to effectively sell their products or services and acquire new customers. By understanding your target customers, choosing the right sales channels, defining your sales process, setting goals, training your sales team, and regularly evaluating your strategy, you can increase your chances of sales success and achieve your business objectives.

Section 5.2
Effective Sales Techniques

In order to successfully acquire customers and drive sales, entrepreneurs must employ effective sales techniques. These techniques are essential for building relationships with potential customers, understanding their needs, and ultimately convincing them to make a purchase. In this section, we will explore some key strategies and tactics that can help entrepreneurs improve their sales performance.

One important sales technique is active listening. By actively listening to customers, entrepreneurs can gain valuable insights into their needs, preferences, and pain points. This allows them to tailor their sales approach and offer personalized solutions that meet the customer's specific requirements. Active listening involves paying close attention to what the customer is saying, asking clarifying questions, and demonstrating empathy and understanding.

Another effective sales technique is building rapport and establishing trust. Customers are more likely to buy from someone they trust and feel comfortable with. Entrepreneurs can build rapport by being genuine, friendly, and approachable. They should strive to create a positive first impression and maintain a professional demeanor throughout the sales process. Building trust also involves delivering on promises, being transparent and honest, and providing excellent customer service.

Effective sales techniques also involve effective communication. Entrepreneurs should be able to clearly articulate the value and benefits of their products or services. They should be able to explain how their offerings can solve the customer's problems or meet their needs. This requires strong communication skills, including the ability to convey complex information in a simple and understandable manner. Entrepreneurs should also be skilled at handling objections and addressing any concerns or doubts the customer may have.

In addition to effective communication, entrepreneurs should also be skilled at negotiation. Negotiation is a crucial sales technique that allows entrepreneurs to reach mutually beneficial agreements with customers. This involves finding common ground, understanding the customer's priorities, and finding creative solutions that meet both parties' needs. Entrepreneurs should be confident and assertive during negotiations, while also being willing to compromise and find win-win solutions.

Furthermore, entrepreneurs should be proactive in their sales approach. Instead of waiting for customers to come to them, they should actively seek out potential leads and opportunities. This can involve networking, attending industry events, leveraging social media, and reaching out to potential customers directly. By taking a proactive approach, entrepreneurs can expand their customer base and increase their sales opportunities.

Lastly, effective sales techniques require persistence and resilience. Not every sales interaction will result in a sale, and entrepreneurs must be prepared for rejection and setbacks. It is important to view each rejection as a learning opportunity and to persistently follow up with potential customers. By staying resilient and maintaining a positive mindset, entrepreneurs can overcome obstacles and ultimately achieve sales success.

In conclusion, effective sales techniques are crucial for entrepreneurs looking to acquire customers and drive sales. By actively listening, building rapport, communicating effectively, negotiating skillfully, being proactive, and staying resilient, entrepreneurs can improve their sales performance and achieve their business goals.

Section 5.3
Building Relationships with Customers

Building strong relationships with customers is essential for the long-term success of any business. When customers feel valued and appreciated, they are more likely to become loyal advocates and repeat buyers. In this section, we will explore strategies for building and nurturing relationships with customers.

One of the first steps in building relationships with customers is to truly understand their needs and preferences. This requires active listening and effective communication. Take the time to engage with your customers, ask questions, and gather feedback. By understanding their pain points and desires, you can tailor your products or services to better meet their expectations.

Another important aspect of building relationships with customers is providing exceptional customer service. Respond promptly to inquiries and resolve any issues or concerns in a timely manner. Show empathy and understanding, and go above and beyond to exceed customer expectations. By providing a positive experience, you can create a strong foundation for a long-lasting relationship.

Personalization is key when it comes to building relationships with customers. Treat each customer as an individual and tailor your interactions accordingly. Use customer data and insights to personalize your marketing messages, offers, and recommendations. By showing that you understand and value each customer's unique needs, you can foster a deeper connection and build trust.

Building relationships with customers also involves staying in touch and maintaining regular communication. Keep your customers informed about new products, promotions, and updates through email newsletters, social media, or other channels. Regularly reach out to check in on their satisfaction and offer support. By staying top of mind, you can strengthen the relationship and encourage repeat business.

In addition to proactive communication, it is important to actively seek feedback from your customers. Conduct surveys, hold focus groups, or use other methods to gather insights on their experience with your business. Use this feedback to continuously improve your products, services, and overall customer experience. By involving customers in the process, you show that their opinions matter and that you are committed to their satisfaction.

Building relationships with customers is not a one-time effort, but an ongoing process. Continuously nurture and strengthen these relationships by showing appreciation and gratitude. Offer exclusive discounts or rewards to loyal customers, send personalized thank-you notes, or host customer appreciation events. By going the extra mile to show your customers that they are valued, you can foster loyalty and advocacy.

In conclusion, building relationships with customers is a crucial aspect of sales and customer acquisition. By understanding their needs, providing exceptional customer service, personalizing interactions, staying in touch, seeking feedback, and showing appreciation, you can create strong and lasting relationships with your customers. These relationships will not only lead to repeat business but also to positive word-of-mouth referrals and a thriving customer base.

Section 5.4
Customer Acquisition and Retention

Customer acquisition and retention are crucial aspects of building a successful business. While acquiring new customers is important for growth, retaining existing customers is equally essential for long-term sustainability. In this section, we will explore strategies and techniques to effectively acquire and retain customers.

To acquire new customers, it is essential to have a clear understanding of your target audience. Conducting market research and analysis will help you identify the needs and preferences of your potential customers. By understanding their pain points and desires, you can tailor your marketing messages and offerings to resonate with them.

Once you have identified your target customers, it is important to develop a comprehensive marketing strategy. This strategy should include various channels and tactics to reach your audience effectively. Utilizing targeted marketing campaigns, such as email marketing, social media advertising, and content marketing, can help you attract the attention of potential customers and drive them towards making a purchase.

In addition to marketing efforts, building relationships with customers is crucial for customer acquisition. Providing exceptional customer service and personalized experiences can leave a lasting impression on your customers. By going above and beyond to meet their needs and expectations, you can create loyal customers who are more likely to refer your business to others.

While acquiring new customers is important, retaining existing customers is equally vital. Customer retention not only leads to repeat business but also helps in building a strong brand reputation. To retain customers, it is important to focus on delivering value consistently. This can be achieved by providing high-quality products or services, offering exclusive discounts or rewards to loyal customers, and maintaining open lines of communication.

Another effective strategy for customer retention is to actively seek feedback from your customers. By listening to their concerns and suggestions, you can continuously improve your offerings and address any issues promptly. This not only shows your commitment to customer satisfaction but also helps in building trust and loyalty.

Implementing a customer loyalty program can also be beneficial for customer retention. By offering incentives and rewards to repeat customers, you can encourage them to continue doing business with you. This can be in the form of discounts, exclusive access to new products or services, or personalized offers based on their preferences.

In conclusion, customer acquisition and retention are essential for the success of any business. By understanding your target audience, developing a comprehensive marketing strategy, and focusing on delivering value consistently, you can effectively acquire and retain customers. Building strong relationships, seeking feedback, and implementing customer loyalty programs are key strategies to ensure customer satisfaction and long-term business growth.

Section 5.5
Upselling and Cross-Selling

Upselling and cross-selling are powerful techniques that can significantly increase revenue and customer satisfaction. Upselling involves persuading customers to purchase a higher-priced product or service than the one they initially intended to buy. Cross-selling, on the other hand, involves offering complementary or related products or services to enhance the customer's overall experience.

One of the key benefits of upselling and cross-selling is that they allow businesses to maximize the value of each customer transaction. By offering additional products or services that align with the customer's needs and preferences, businesses can increase their average order value and ultimately boost their bottom line.

To effectively upsell and cross-sell, it is crucial to have a deep understanding of your customers and their buying habits. This requires gathering and analyzing data about their past purchases, preferences, and behavior. By leveraging this information, you can identify opportunities to recommend relevant products or services that will enhance the customer's experience or solve their problems.

When implementing upselling and cross-selling strategies, it is important to strike a balance between providing value to the customer and avoiding pushy or aggressive sales tactics. The goal is to genuinely help the customer make informed decisions that align with their needs and preferences. By focusing on the customer's best interests, businesses can build trust and loyalty, leading to long-term customer relationships.

One effective approach to upselling is to highlight the additional benefits or features of a higher-priced product or service. By demonstrating how the upgraded option can better meet the customer's needs or provide a superior experience, you can increase the perceived value and justify the higher price point. It is important to clearly communicate these benefits and address any potential objections or concerns the customer may have. Cross-selling, on the other hand, involves offering complementary or related products or services that enhance the customer's overall experience. This can be done by suggesting items that are commonly purchased together or by recommending products or services that complement the customer's initial purchase. By showcasing the value and convenience of these additional offerings, businesses can increase the customer's satisfaction and encourage repeat purchases.

To effectively implement upselling and cross-selling strategies, businesses should train their sales and customer service teams to identify opportunities and make relevant recommendations. This requires providing them with comprehensive product knowledge and sales training, as well as empowering them to make personalized recommendations based on the customer's specific needs and preferences.

In conclusion, upselling and cross-selling are valuable techniques that can significantly impact a business's sales and customer acquisition efforts. By understanding the customer's needs, providing value, and making relevant recommendations, businesses can increase their revenue, enhance the customer's experience, and build long-term customer relationships.

Section 5.6

Providing Exceptional Customer Service

Exceptional customer service is a crucial aspect of any successful business. It goes beyond simply selling a product or service; it involves building strong relationships with customers and ensuring their satisfaction throughout their entire journey with your company. By providing exceptional customer service, you not only increase customer loyalty and retention but also attract new customers through positive word-of-mouth.

One key element of exceptional customer service is effective communication. It is important to listen to your customers, understand their needs, and respond promptly and appropriately. Whether it's through phone calls, emails, or in-person interactions, make sure your team is trained to communicate clearly and professionally, addressing any concerns or questions that may arise.

Another aspect of exceptional customer service is going above and beyond to exceed customer expectations. This can be achieved by offering personalized experiences, anticipating customer needs, and providing solutions that are tailored to their specific requirements. By demonstrating that you genuinely care about your customers and their satisfaction, you create a positive impression that sets you apart from your competitors.

Timeliness is also crucial in providing exceptional customer service. Responding to customer inquiries and resolving issues in a timely manner shows that you value their time and are committed to providing a seamless experience. Implementing efficient systems and processes to handle customer requests and complaints can help ensure that no customer is left waiting for a resolution.

Training your team to handle difficult situations and challenging customers is another important aspect of exceptional customer service. Empowering your employees to handle complaints and resolve issues with empathy and professionalism can turn a potentially negative experience into a positive one. By providing ongoing training and support, you equip your team with the skills and knowledge needed to handle any customer service situation effectively.

Lastly, gathering feedback from your customers is essential in continuously improving your customer service. Implementing surveys, feedback forms, or even conducting one-on-one interviews can provide valuable insights into areas where you can enhance your customer service efforts. Actively seeking feedback and taking action on it demonstrates your commitment to providing exceptional customer service and shows that you value your customers' opinions.

In conclusion, providing exceptional customer service is a vital component of successful sales and customer acquisition. By focusing on effective communication, exceeding customer expectations, being timely in your responses, training your team, and actively seeking feedback, you can create a customer-centric culture that sets your business apart. Remember, exceptional customer service not only leads to customer satisfaction and loyalty but also contributes to the long-term success and growth of your business.

Chapter 6
Financial Management and Planning

Section 6.1
Budgeting and Forecasting

Budgeting and forecasting are essential components of effective financial management and planning for entrepreneurs. By creating a budget, entrepreneurs can allocate resources and set financial goals for their business. A budget serves as a roadmap, guiding decision-making and ensuring that financial resources are used efficiently and effectively.

To create a budget, entrepreneurs must first identify their sources of income and expenses. This includes revenue from sales, investments, and any other sources, as well as costs such as rent, salaries, marketing expenses, and supplies. By categorizing and organizing these income and expense items, entrepreneurs can gain a clear understanding of their financial situation.

Once the income and expenses are identified, entrepreneurs can then set financial goals and allocate resources accordingly. This involves determining how much money should be allocated to each expense category and setting targets for revenue generation. By setting realistic and achievable goals, entrepreneurs can ensure that their budget is aligned with their overall business objectives.

Forecasting, on the other hand, involves predicting future financial outcomes based on historical data and market trends. By analyzing past financial performance and market conditions, entrepreneurs can make informed projections about their business's future financial position. This allows them to anticipate potential challenges and opportunities and make strategic decisions accordingly.

When creating a budget and forecasting, it is important for entrepreneurs to consider various factors that may impact their financial situation. This includes changes in market conditions, industry trends, and economic factors. By staying informed and regularly reviewing and updating their budget and forecasts, entrepreneurs can adapt their financial plans to changing circumstances and make necessary adjustments.

In addition to budgeting and forecasting, entrepreneurs should also monitor and track their financial performance regularly. This involves comparing actual financial results against the budget and forecasts, identifying any variances, and taking corrective actions if necessary. By regularly reviewing their financial performance, entrepreneurs can ensure that they are on track to achieve their financial goals and make informed decisions to improve their business's financial health.

Overall, budgeting and forecasting are crucial tools for entrepreneurs to effectively manage their finances and plan for the future. By creating a budget, setting financial goals, and making informed projections, entrepreneurs can make strategic decisions, allocate resources efficiently, and ensure the long-term sustainability and success of their business.

Section 6.2
Managing Cash Flow

Managing cash flow is a critical aspect of financial management for entrepreneurs. Cash flow refers to the movement of money in and out of a business, including the inflow of revenue and the outflow of expenses. Effectively managing cash flow is essential for the smooth operation and long-term sustainability of a business.

One of the key challenges entrepreneurs face is ensuring that there is enough cash available to cover day-to-day expenses, such as paying suppliers, employees, and other operational costs. Without proper cash flow management, a business may struggle to meet its financial obligations, leading to cash shortages and potential financial distress.

To effectively manage cash flow, entrepreneurs should

105

start by creating a cash flow forecast. This involves projecting the expected inflows and outflows of cash over a specific period, typically on a monthly or quarterly basis. By forecasting cash flow, entrepreneurs can anticipate potential cash shortfalls or surpluses and take proactive measures to address them.

In addition to forecasting, entrepreneurs should also closely monitor their actual cash flow on an ongoing basis. This involves regularly reviewing and updating the cash flow forecast based on actual cash inflows and outflows. By comparing the forecasted cash flow with the actual cash flow, entrepreneurs can identify any discrepancies and take corrective actions if necessary.

To improve cash flow management, entrepreneurs can implement several strategies. One strategy is to negotiate favorable payment terms with suppliers, such as extended payment terms or discounts for early payment. This can help to delay cash outflows and improve the timing of cash inflows.

Another strategy is to closely manage accounts receivable and accounts payable. Entrepreneurs should strive to collect payments from customers as quickly as possible and negotiate favorable payment terms with suppliers. By reducing the time it takes to collect payments and extending the time it takes to make payments, entrepreneurs can improve cash flow.

Entrepreneurs should also consider implementing effective inventory management practices. Excess inventory ties up cash and can lead to cash flow problems. By closely monitoring inventory levels and optimizing the ordering and production processes, entrepreneurs can reduce inventory holding costs and improve cash flow.

Furthermore, entrepreneurs should regularly review their expenses and identify areas where costs can be reduced or eliminated. By cutting unnecessary expenses and optimizing spending, entrepreneurs can free up cash and improve cash flow.

In conclusion, managing cash flow is crucial for the financial health and success of a business. By creating a cash flow forecast, monitoring actual cash flow, and implementing effective cash flow management strategies, entrepreneurs can ensure that their business has enough cash to meet its financial obligations and support its growth and development.

Section 6.3
Pricing Strategies

Pricing strategies play a crucial role in the financial management and planning of a business. Determining the right price for your products or services is essential for generating revenue and maximizing profitability. In this section, we will explore various pricing strategies that successful entrepreneurs employ to effectively price their offerings.

One common pricing strategy is cost-based pricing. This approach involves calculating the total cost of producing a product or delivering a service and adding a desired profit margin on top. By considering the expenses incurred in manufacturing, labor, materials, and overhead costs, entrepreneurs can determine a price that covers their expenses and generates a profit. Cost-based pricing provides a straightforward method for setting prices, especially for businesses with stable and predictable costs.

Another pricing strategy is value-based pricing. This approach focuses on the perceived value of a product or service to customers. Instead of solely considering production costs, entrepreneurs assess the value that their offerings provide to customers and price accordingly. By understanding the benefits and unique selling points of their products or services, entrepreneurs can set prices that align with the perceived value and willingness of customers to pay. Value-based pricing allows businesses to capture a higher price point for their offerings, especially if they can effectively communicate the value proposition to customers.

Dynamic pricing is a strategy that involves adjusting prices based on market demand and other external factors. This approach allows entrepreneurs to optimize their pricing in real-time, taking advantage of fluctuations in demand and supply. For example, during periods of high demand, prices can be increased to maximize revenue, while during periods of low demand, prices can be lowered to stimulate sales. Dynamic pricing requires businesses to have the ability to monitor market conditions and adjust prices accordingly, often leveraging technology and data analytics.

Penetration pricing is a strategy commonly used by businesses entering a new market or launching a new product. The goal of penetration pricing is to attract customers by offering a lower price compared to competitors. This strategy aims to gain market share and create brand awareness, with the intention of increasing prices once the business has established a customer base. Penetration pricing can be an effective way to quickly gain traction in a competitive market, but it requires careful planning to ensure that the initial lower prices are sustainable in the long term.

Price skimming is a strategy that involves setting a high initial price for a new product or service and gradually lowering it over time. This approach is often used for innovative or unique offerings that have a limited target market willing to pay a premium price. By initially targeting early adopters and price-insensitive customers, entrepreneurs can capture maximum revenue before gradually reducing prices to attract a broader customer base. Price skimming can be an effective strategy for maximizing profits in the early stages of a product or service lifecycle.

In conclusion, pricing strategies are an integral part of financial management and planning for entrepreneurs. By carefully considering factors such as costs, value, market demand, and competition, entrepreneurs can determine the most appropriate pricing strategy for their business. Whether it's cost-based pricing, value-based pricing, dynamic pricing, penetration pricing, or price skimming, selecting the right pricing strategy can significantly impact a business's profitability and success.

Section 6.4
Financial Analysis and Reporting

Financial analysis and reporting are crucial components of effective financial management and planning. By analyzing financial data and generating reports, entrepreneurs can gain valuable insights into the financial health of their business and make informed decisions to drive growth and profitability.

One key aspect of financial analysis is the examination of financial statements, such as the income statement, balance sheet, and cash flow statement. These statements provide a comprehensive overview of the company's financial performance, including revenue, expenses, assets, liabilities, and cash flow. By analyzing these statements, entrepreneurs can assess the profitability, liquidity, and solvency of their business.

Ratio analysis is another important tool in financial

analysis. Ratios help entrepreneurs evaluate the financial performance and efficiency of their business by comparing different financial variables. Common ratios include profitability ratios (such as gross profit margin and net profit margin), liquidity ratios (such as current ratio and quick ratio), and leverage ratios (such as debt-to-equity ratio and interest coverage ratio). By analyzing these ratios, entrepreneurs can identify areas of strength and weakness in their financial management and make necessary adjustments.

Financial analysis also involves benchmarking, which is the process of comparing a company's financial performance to industry standards or competitors. By benchmarking, entrepreneurs can assess how their business measures up against others in terms of profitability, efficiency, and financial stability. This analysis can help identify areas for improvement and guide strategic decision-making.

In addition to financial analysis, entrepreneurs must also focus on financial reporting. Financial reports provide a summary of the company's financial performance and position, and they are essential for stakeholders such as investors, lenders, and regulatory authorities. Common financial reports include the annual report, which provides a comprehensive overview of the company's financial performance and operations, and the quarterly report, which provides updates on the company's financial results and progress towards goals.

When preparing financial reports, entrepreneurs must ensure accuracy, transparency, and compliance with accounting standards and regulations. They should also consider the needs and expectations of different stakeholders and tailor the reports accordingly. Effective financial reporting not only helps entrepreneurs communicate the financial health of their business but also builds trust and credibility with stakeholders.

To enhance financial analysis and reporting, entrepreneurs can leverage technology and financial management software. These tools automate data collection, analysis, and reporting processes, saving time and improving accuracy. They also provide real-time insights and customizable reports, enabling entrepreneurs to make timely and informed financial decisions.

In conclusion, financial analysis and reporting are essential for effective financial management and planning. By analyzing financial statements, using ratios, benchmarking, and preparing accurate and transparent financial reports, entrepreneurs can gain valuable insights into their business's financial health and make informed decisions to drive growth and profitability. Leveraging technology and financial management software can further enhance these processes, enabling entrepreneurs to stay on top of their finances and achieve long-term success

Section 6.5
Tax Planning and Compliance

Tax planning and compliance are crucial aspects of financial management for entrepreneurs. Understanding and effectively managing taxes can help businesses optimize their financial resources and ensure compliance with legal requirements. In this section, we will explore the importance of tax planning, strategies for minimizing tax liabilities, and the significance of complying with tax regulations.

Tax planning involves analyzing the tax implications of various business decisions and structuring them in a way that minimizes tax liabilities. By strategically planning their taxes, entrepreneurs can legally reduce their tax burden and maximize their after-tax profits. This requires a thorough understanding of tax laws and regulations, as well as staying updated on any changes or updates that may affect the business.

One key aspect of tax planning is identifying and utilizing available tax deductions, credits, and exemptions. Entrepreneurs should be aware of the tax incentives and benefits offered by the government for specific industries or activities. By taking advantage of these incentives, businesses can lower their taxable income and potentially save a significant amount of money.

Another important consideration in tax planning is the choice of business structure. Different business structures, such as sole proprietorships, partnerships, corporations, or limited liability companies, have different tax implications. Entrepreneurs should carefully evaluate the tax advantages and disadvantages of each structure and choose the one that aligns with their business goals and objectives.

Compliance with tax regulations is equally important for entrepreneurs. Failing to comply with tax laws can result in penalties, fines, and even legal consequences. It is essential to maintain accurate and up-to-date financial records, including income, expenses, and deductions, to ensure accurate reporting and filing of tax returns.

To ensure compliance, entrepreneurs should stay informed about the tax filing deadlines and requirements specific to their business. This includes understanding the different types of taxes applicable to their industry, such as income tax, sales tax, payroll tax, and any other relevant taxes. Seeking professional advice from tax experts or hiring a qualified accountant can be beneficial in navigating the complexities of tax compliance.

In addition to tax planning and compliance, entrepreneurs should also consider the potential impact of tax changes on their business. Tax laws and regulations are subject to change, and entrepreneurs need to stay informed about any updates that may affect their tax liabilities. This may involve regularly reviewing tax legislation, consulting with tax professionals, and adjusting their tax strategies accordingly.

In conclusion, tax planning and compliance are essential components of financial management for entrepreneurs. By strategically planning their taxes and ensuring compliance with tax regulations, businesses can optimize their financial resources, minimize tax liabilities, and avoid legal consequences. It is crucial for entrepreneurs to stay informed about tax laws, seek professional advice when needed, and adapt their tax strategies to changes in the tax landscape.

Section 6.6
Seeking Professional Financial Advice

Seeking professional financial advice is crucial for entrepreneurs who want to effectively manage their finances and make informed decisions. While entrepreneurs may have a good understanding of their business and industry, they may not possess the expertise or knowledge required to navigate complex financial matters.

Professional financial advisors can provide valuable insights and guidance on various aspects of financial management, including budgeting, forecasting, cash flow management, pricing strategies, financial analysis, and tax planning. They have the expertise to analyze financial data, identify potential risks, and develop strategies to mitigate them.

One of the key benefits of seeking professional financial advice is gaining access to a wealth of knowledge and experience. Financial advisors have a deep understanding of financial markets, regulations, and industry trends. They can provide entrepreneurs with valuable insights into market conditions, investment opportunities, and potential risks. This knowledge can help entrepreneurs make informed decisions and avoid costly mistakes.

Another advantage of working with a financial advisor is the ability to develop a comprehensive financial plan. A financial plan outlines the entrepreneur's financial goals and the strategies to achieve them. It includes a budget, cash flow projections, investment plans, and risk management strategies. A financial advisor can help entrepreneurs develop a realistic and achievable financial plan tailored to their specific business needs and objectives.

Financial advisors can also assist entrepreneurs in managing their cash flow effectively. Cash flow management is crucial for the survival and growth of a business. A financial advisor can help entrepreneurs analyze their cash flow patterns, identify potential cash flow gaps, and develop strategies to address them. They can also provide advice on managing working capital, optimizing inventory levels, and negotiating favorable payment terms with suppliers.

In addition to financial planning and cash flow management, financial advisors can provide guidance on pricing strategies. Determining the right pricing strategy is essential for profitability and competitiveness. A financial advisor can help entrepreneurs analyze their costs, assess market demand, and determine optimal pricing levels. They can also provide insights into pricing strategies used by competitors and help entrepreneurs position their products or services effectively in the market.

Furthermore, financial advisors can assist entrepreneurs in conducting financial analysis and reporting. They can help entrepreneurs analyze financial statements, identify key performance indicators, and develop meaningful financial reports. This analysis can provide entrepreneurs with a clear understanding of their business's financial health and performance, enabling them to make data-driven decisions.

Lastly, financial advisors can provide guidance on tax

planning and compliance. Tax planning is essential for minimizing tax liabilities and ensuring compliance with tax laws and regulations. A financial advisor can help entrepreneurs identify tax-saving opportunities, optimize their tax structure, and ensure timely and accurate tax filings. They can also keep entrepreneurs informed about changes in tax laws and regulations that may impact their business.

In conclusion, seeking professional financial advice is crucial for entrepreneurs to effectively manage their finances and make informed decisions. Financial advisors can provide valuable insights and guidance on various aspects of financial management, including budgeting, forecasting, cash flow management, pricing strategies, financial analysis, and tax planning. Their expertise and knowledge can help entrepreneurs develop comprehensive financial plans, manage cash flow effectively, determine optimal pricing strategies, conduct financial analysis and reporting, and ensure tax compliance. By working with a financial advisor, entrepreneurs can enhance their financial management capabilities and increase their chances of long-term business success.

Chapter 7
Scaling and Growth Strategies

Section 7.1
Identifying Growth Opportunities

Identifying growth opportunities is a crucial step in scaling and expanding your business. It involves recognizing potential areas for growth and developing strategies to capitalize on them. By identifying these opportunities, you can position your business for long-term success and stay ahead of the competition.

One way to identify growth opportunities is through market research and analysis. This involves studying market trends, customer preferences, and industry developments to uncover potential areas of growth. By understanding the needs and desires of your target customers, you can identify gaps in the market that your business can fill. This could involve developing new

The Secrets of Successful Entrepreneurs

products or services, entering new markets, or targeting underserved customer segments.

Another way to identify growth opportunities is by analyzing your competitors. By studying their strategies, strengths, and weaknesses, you can identify areas where your business can differentiate itself and gain a competitive advantage. This could involve offering unique features or benefits, improving customer service, or finding ways to lower costs and increase efficiency.

Spotting trends and innovations is also key to identifying growth opportunities. By staying up-to-date with industry developments and emerging technologies, you can identify new ways to meet customer needs and stay ahead of the curve. This could involve adopting new technologies, exploring new distribution channels, or leveraging emerging trends to create innovative products or services.

Evaluating potential risks is an important part of identifying growth opportunities. While growth can bring many benefits, it also comes with risks and challenges. By assessing the potential risks associated with each growth opportunity, you can develop strategies to mitigate them and ensure a successful expansion. This could involve conducting a thorough risk analysis, developing contingency plans, or seeking expert advice to navigate potential obstacles.

In conclusion, identifying growth opportunities is essential for scaling and expanding your business. By conducting market research, analyzing competitors, spotting trends, and evaluating risks, you can uncover potential areas for growth and develop strategies to capitalize on them. By staying proactive and adaptable, you can position your business for long-term success and achieve sustainable growth.

Section 7.2

Expanding into New Markets

Expanding into new markets is a crucial step for entrepreneurs looking to scale and grow their businesses. By entering new markets, entrepreneurs can tap into untapped customer segments, increase their customer base, and diversify their revenue streams. However, expanding into new markets requires careful planning and execution to ensure success.

One of the first steps in expanding into new markets is conducting thorough market research. This involves analyzing the target market's demographics, purchasing behaviors, and preferences. By understanding the needs and wants of the new market, entrepreneurs can tailor their products or services to meet the specific demands of the customers.

Once the market research is complete, entrepreneurs should develop a comprehensive market entry strategy. This strategy should outline the approach to entering the new market, including the marketing and sales tactics to be employed. It is important to consider factors such as pricing, distribution channels, and promotional activities when formulating the market entry strategy.

Another important aspect of expanding into new markets is building relationships with local partners or distributors. These partners can provide valuable insights into the local market, help navigate cultural differences, and assist with distribution and logistics. Collaborating with local partners can also help establish credibility and trust with the new market's customers.

In addition to building relationships with local partners, entrepreneurs should also consider adapting their products or services to suit the preferences and needs of the new market. This may involve making modifications to the product design, packaging, or even the pricing strategy. By tailoring the offering to the new market, entrepreneurs can increase the chances of success and acceptance by the target customers.

Furthermore, entrepreneurs should allocate sufficient resources and budget for the expansion into new markets. This includes investing in marketing and promotional activities, hiring local staff or representatives, and setting up distribution channels. Adequate resources and budget allocation are essential to ensure a smooth and successful entry into the new market.

Once the expansion into a new market is underway, it is important to continuously monitor and evaluate the performance. This involves tracking key performance indicators, such as sales growth, customer feedback, and market share. By regularly assessing the progress, entrepreneurs can make necessary adjustments and improvements to optimize their presence in the new market.

Expanding into new markets can be a challenging yet rewarding endeavor for entrepreneurs. It requires careful planning, market research, and adaptation to the local market. By following a strategic approach and leveraging local partnerships, entrepreneurs can successfully enter new markets and achieve sustainable growth for their businesses.

Section 7.3
Strategic Partnerships and Alliances

Strategic partnerships and alliances play a crucial role in the scaling and growth of a business. By forming strategic partnerships, entrepreneurs can leverage the strengths and resources of other companies to expand their reach, access new markets, and drive innovation. These partnerships can take various forms, such as joint ventures, collaborations, or formal alliances.

One of the key benefits of strategic partnerships is the ability to tap into the expertise and knowledge of other companies. By partnering with organizations that have complementary skills and capabilities, entrepreneurs can access specialized knowledge and experience that may not be available within their own company. This can help them overcome challenges, develop new products or services, and enter new markets more effectively.

Strategic partnerships also provide access to new customer segments and distribution channels. By partnering with companies that have an established customer base or distribution network, entrepreneurs can quickly expand their reach and increase their market share. This can be particularly beneficial for startups or small businesses that may not have the resources or brand recognition to penetrate new markets on their own.

Furthermore, strategic partnerships can lead to cost savings and efficiencies. By sharing resources, infrastructure, or research and development costs, companies can reduce their expenses and improve their profitability. This can be especially valuable for businesses operating in highly competitive industries or facing financial constraints.

In addition to these tangible benefits, strategic partnerships can also enhance a company's reputation and credibility. By aligning with reputable and well-established organizations, entrepreneurs can gain the trust and confidence of customers, investors, and other stakeholders. This can open doors to new opportunities, attract top talent, and strengthen the overall brand image of the business.

However, it is important for entrepreneurs to approach strategic partnerships with careful consideration and due diligence. It is crucial to assess the compatibility of potential partners in terms of values, goals, and culture.

A misalignment in these areas can lead to conflicts and hinder the success of the partnership. It is also important to establish clear communication channels, roles, and responsibilities to ensure effective collaboration and decision-making.

To identify potential strategic partners, entrepreneurs should conduct thorough market research and analysis. They should identify companies that have complementary strengths, similar target customers, or a shared vision for growth. Networking events, industry conferences, and trade associations can be valuable sources for connecting with potential partners.

Once a strategic partnership is established, it is important to nurture and maintain the relationship. Regular communication, collaboration, and mutual support are essential for the success of the partnership. Entrepreneurs should also regularly evaluate the performance and impact of the partnership to ensure that it continues to align with their business objectives and contributes to their growth strategy.

In conclusion, strategic partnerships and alliances are powerful tools for scaling and growing a business. By leveraging the strengths and resources of other companies, entrepreneurs can access new markets, drive innovation, and achieve sustainable growth. However, it is important to approach partnerships with careful consideration and establish clear communication and collaboration channels. With the right strategic partnerships in place, entrepreneurs can accelerate their growth and achieve long-term success.

Section 7.4
Franchising and Licensing

Franchising and licensing are two popular strategies for scaling and expanding a business. These approaches allow entrepreneurs to leverage their successful business model, brand, and intellectual property to reach new markets and customers without the need for significant capital investment or direct operational involvement.

Franchising involves granting the rights to operate a business under a well-established brand and proven system to independent individuals or entities known as franchisees. The franchisor provides the franchisee with support, training, and ongoing assistance in exchange for fees and royalties. This arrangement allows the franchisor to expand their business rapidly while sharing the risks and responsibilities with the franchisees.

One of the key advantages of franchising is the ability to tap into the local knowledge and expertise of franchisees. They have a vested interest in the success of their individual franchise locations, which often leads to higher levels of dedication and customer service. Franchising also allows for rapid geographic expansion, as franchisees can open new locations in different regions or even countries.

However, franchising also comes with its challenges. Franchisor need to ensure that their business model is easily replicable and can be effectively communicated to franchisees. They must also provide ongoing support and training to maintain consistency across all franchise locations. Additionally, franchisors need to carefully select and vet potential franchisees to ensure they align with the brand's values and standards.

Licensing, on the other hand, involves granting the rights to use a company's intellectual property, such as trademarks, patents, or copyrights, to another party in exchange for royalties or licensing fees. This allows the licensee to produce and sell products or services using the licensed intellectual property. Licensing is commonly used in industries such as technology, entertainment, and consumer goods.

Licensing offers several benefits for businesses looking to scale and grow. It allows them to generate additional revenue streams without the need for significant investment in production or distribution. Licensing also enables businesses to enter new markets or expand their product offerings through partnerships with established companies that have existing distribution networks or expertise in specific markets.

However, licensing also requires careful management and protection of intellectual property. Businesses must ensure that their licensed intellectual property is used appropriately and that licensees adhere to quality standards and brand guidelines. Licensing agreements should be well-drafted and include provisions for monitoring and enforcing compliance.

Both franchising and licensing can be effective strategies for scaling and growing a business. The choice between the two depends on factors such as the nature of the business, its growth objectives, and the level of control the entrepreneur wants to maintain. It is important for entrepreneurs to thoroughly evaluate the pros and cons of each strategy and seek professional advice when considering franchising or licensing as part of their growth plans.

Section 7.5
Product and Service Diversification

Product and service diversification is a crucial strategy for entrepreneurs looking to scale and grow their businesses. By expanding the range of products or services offered, entrepreneurs can tap into new markets, attract a wider customer base, and increase revenue streams.

One of the key benefits of product and service diversification is the ability to mitigate risks associated with relying too heavily on a single product or service. By offering a variety of products or services, entrepreneurs can spread their risk and reduce their vulnerability to market fluctuations or changes in customer preferences. This diversification can provide a buffer against economic downturns or industry-specific challenges, ensuring the long-term sustainability of the business.

Moreover, product and service diversification allows entrepreneurs to capitalize on emerging trends and customer demands. By staying attuned to market needs and preferences, entrepreneurs can identify opportunities to expand their offerings and meet the evolving needs of their target customers. This proactive approach to diversification can help businesses stay ahead of the competition and maintain a competitive edge in the market.

When considering product and service diversification, entrepreneurs should conduct thorough market research to identify gaps or untapped opportunities. This research should involve analyzing customer needs, preferences, and purchasing behaviors, as well as studying industry trends and competitor offerings. By understanding the market landscape, entrepreneurs can make informed decisions about which products or services to introduce or expand upon.

It is important for entrepreneurs to ensure that any new products or services align with their existing brand identity and values. Consistency in branding and messaging is crucial for maintaining customer trust and loyalty. Entrepreneurs should carefully evaluate how the new offerings fit within their overall business strategy and how they can leverage their existing customer base to drive adoption and sales.

Implementing product and service diversification requires careful planning and execution. Entrepreneurs should consider factors such as production capabilities, supply chain management, and resource allocation when expanding their offerings. It may be necessary to invest in additional resources, such as equipment, technology, or talent, to support the diversification efforts. Entrepreneurs should also develop a marketing and sales strategy to effectively promote and sell the new products or services to their target audience.

Monitoring and evaluating the performance of the diversified products or services is essential to ensure their success. Entrepreneurs should track key metrics, such as sales volume, customer feedback, and profitability, to assess the impact of the diversification strategy. This data can help entrepreneurs make informed decisions about further refining or expanding their product and service offerings.

In conclusion, product and service diversification is a powerful strategy for entrepreneurs seeking to scale and grow their businesses. By expanding their offerings, entrepreneurs can mitigate risks, tap into new markets, and meet the evolving needs of their customers. However, successful diversification requires careful planning, market research, and alignment with the overall business strategy. With the right approach, entrepreneurs can leverage product and service diversification to drive sustainable growth and long-term success.

Section 7.6
Managing Rapid Growth and Scaling Challenges

Managing rapid growth and scaling challenges is a crucial aspect of building a thriving business. While experiencing rapid growth can be exciting, it also brings its own set of challenges that entrepreneurs must navigate effectively. In this section, we will explore strategies and best practices for managing rapid growth and overcoming scaling challenges.

One of the key challenges that entrepreneurs face when experiencing rapid growth is maintaining operational efficiency. As the business expands, it becomes essential to streamline processes and optimize workflow to ensure that the increased demand can be met effectively. This may involve reevaluating and redesigning operational processes, implementing automation and technology solutions, and continuously monitoring and improving efficiency.

Another important aspect of managing rapid growth is scaling the team effectively. As the business grows, it is crucial to hire the right talent and build a high-performing team that can support the increased workload. This may involve assessing the current team's capabilities and identifying any skill gaps that need to be filled. Additionally, implementing effective recruitment and onboarding processes can help ensure that new hires are aligned with the company's values and goals.

Financial management is also a critical factor in managing rapid growth. As the business expands, it is essential to closely monitor cash flow, budgeting, and forecasting to ensure that the financial resources are allocated effectively. This may involve seeking professional financial advice, implementing robust financial analysis and reporting systems, and regularly reviewing and adjusting financial strategies to support the growth trajectory.

Communication and collaboration become even more crucial during periods of rapid growth. As the business expands, it is essential to maintain clear and open lines of communication across all levels of the organization. This includes regular team meetings, setting clear expectations, and fostering a culture of transparency and accountability. Additionally, effective collaboration between different departments and teams can help ensure that everyone is aligned and working towards the same goals.

Managing rapid growth also requires a proactive approach to risk management. As the business expands, it becomes more exposed to various risks and uncertainties. It is crucial to identify and assess potential risks, develop contingency plans, and regularly review and update risk management strategies. This may involve conducting regular risk assessments, implementing robust risk mitigation measures, and staying informed about industry trends and market changes.

Lastly, maintaining a strong company culture becomes even more important during periods of rapid growth. As the business expands, it is essential to nurture and reinforce the core values and mission that define the company's culture. This includes fostering a positive work environment, encouraging diversity and inclusion, recognizing and rewarding success, and promoting work -life balance. A strong company culture can help attract and retain top talent, foster employee engagement and loyalty, and drive long-term sustainability and success.

In conclusion, managing rapid growth and scaling challenges is a critical aspect of building a thriving business. By focusing on operational efficiency, scaling the team effectively, implementing robust financial management strategies, fostering effective communication and collaboration, proactively managing risks, and nurturing a strong company culture, entrepreneurs can navigate the challenges of rapid growth and position their businesses for long-term sustainability and success.

Chapter 8
Innovation and Adaptation

Section 8.1
Encouraging Creativity and Innovation

Innovation and creativity are essential for the success and growth of any business. In today's rapidly changing business landscape, companies need to constantly adapt and come up with new ideas to stay ahead of the competition. Encouraging creativity and innovation within your organization can lead to breakthroughs, improved processes, and the development of unique products or services.

To foster a culture of creativity and innovation, it is important to create an environment that encourages and rewards new ideas. This can be done by providing employees with the freedom to experiment and take risks, without the fear of failure. Encourage brainstorming sessions and open discussions where everyone's ideas are valued and considered.

Another way to encourage creativity is to provide employees with the necessary resources and tools to explore new ideas. This can include investing in research and development, providing training and development opportunities, and creating spaces for collaboration and experimentation. By giving employees the support they need, you are empowering them to think outside the box and come up with innovative solutions.

It is also important to lead by example and show your own commitment to creativity and innovation. As a leader, you can set the tone for the organization by being open to new ideas, embracing change, and taking calculated risks. By demonstrating your own willingness to try new things, you inspire others to do the same.

In addition to creating a supportive environment, it is important to establish processes and systems that facilitate the implementation of new ideas. This can include setting up innovation teams or committees, creating a feedback loop for idea generation and evaluation, and providing resources for prototyping and testing. By having a structured approach to innovation, you can ensure that ideas are not only generated but also implemented effectively.

Furthermore, it is important to celebrate and recognize creativity and innovation within your organization. This can be done through rewards and incentives for innovative ideas, showcasing success stories, and creating a culture of appreciation for those who contribute to the growth and development of the business. By acknowledging and rewarding creativity, you create a positive feedback loop that encourages further innovation.

In conclusion, encouraging creativity and innovation is crucial for the long-term success and sustainability of any business. By creating an environment that supports and rewards new ideas, providing the necessary resources and tools, leading by example, establishing processes for implementation, and celebrating innovation, you can foster a culture of creativity and innovation within your organization. This will not only drive growth and competitiveness but also attract and retain top talent who thrive in an environment that values and encourages innovation.

Section 8.2
Embracing Technology and Automation

In today's rapidly evolving business landscape, embracing technology and automation is crucial for the success and growth of any entrepreneur. Technology has revolutionized the way businesses operate, allowing for increased efficiency, productivity, and scalability. By leveraging the power of technology, entrepreneurs can streamline their processes, reduce costs, and gain a competitive edge in the market.

One of the key benefits of embracing technology is the ability to automate repetitive tasks. Automation not only saves time but also minimizes the risk of human error. By automating routine processes such as data entry, inventory management, and customer support, entrepreneurs can free up valuable time and resources to focus on more strategic and value-added activities. This not only improves overall productivity but also enhances the customer experience by ensuring faster response times and greater accuracy.

Furthermore, technology enables entrepreneurs to gather and analyze vast amounts of data, providing valuable insights into customer behavior, market trends, and business performance. With the help of advanced analytics tools, entrepreneurs can make data-driven decisions, identify opportunities for growth, and optimize their strategies. By harnessing the power of data, entrepreneurs can gain a deeper understanding of their target audience, personalize their offerings, and deliver a more tailored and relevant customer experience.

Another aspect of embracing technology is the adoption of digital marketing strategies. In today's digital age, having a strong online presence is essential for reaching and engaging with customers. Entrepreneurs can leverage various digital marketing channels such as social media, search engine optimization, and content marketing to promote their products or services, build brand awareness, and attract new customers. Digital marketing allows for targeted and personalized campaigns, enabling entrepreneurs to reach the right audience at the right time with the right message.

Moreover, technology enables entrepreneurs to stay connected and collaborate with their team members, partners, and customers regardless of geographical boundaries. With the advent of communication and collaboration tools such as video conferencing, project management software, and cloud-based storage, entrepreneurs can foster seamless communication, enhance teamwork, and improve overall efficiency. This not only facilitates remote work and flexible work arrangements but also enables entrepreneurs to tap into a global talent pool and expand their business beyond traditional boundaries.

However, embracing technology and automation also comes with its challenges. It requires entrepreneurs to stay updated with the latest technological advancements, invest in the right tools and infrastructure, and ensure the security and privacy of their data. It also requires a mindset shift and a willingness to adapt to new ways of doing business. Entrepreneurs must be open to learning and embracing new technologies, as well as fostering a culture of innovation and continuous improvement within their organizations.

In conclusion, embracing technology and automation is essential for entrepreneurs who want to thrive in today's fast-paced and competitive business environment. By leveraging technology, entrepreneurs can automate repetitive tasks, gather and analyze data, enhance their marketing efforts, and foster seamless communication and collaboration. However, it is important for entrepreneurs to approach technology adoption strategically, ensuring that it aligns with their business goals and values. By embracing technology and staying ahead of the curve, entrepreneurs can position themselves for long-term success and sustainable growth.

Section 8.3
Continuous Learning and Development

Continuous learning and development are essential for entrepreneurs who want to stay ahead in today's rapidly changing business landscape. In order to innovate and adapt to market changes, entrepreneurs must constantly seek new knowledge and skills to enhance their capabilities.

One of the key aspects of continuous learning is staying

updated on industry trends and advancements. This can be done through various means such as attending conferences, workshops, and seminars, as well as reading industry publications and following thought leaders in the field. By staying informed about the latest developments, entrepreneurs can identify new opportunities and potential areas for growth.

In addition to staying updated on industry trends, entrepreneurs should also focus on developing their skills and knowledge in specific areas relevant to their business. This can involve taking courses or certifications, participating in online learning platforms, or seeking mentorship from experienced professionals. By continuously improving their skills, entrepreneurs can enhance their ability to innovate and adapt to changing market demands.

Continuous learning and development also involves fostering a culture of learning within the organization. Entrepreneurs should encourage their employees to pursue professional development opportunities and provide resources and support for their growth. This can include offering training programs, creating mentorship opportunities, and providing access to educational resources.

Furthermore, entrepreneurs should prioritize personal development and self-reflection. This can involve setting aside time for self-assessment, identifying areas for improvement, and creating a plan for personal growth. By continuously investing in their own development, entrepreneurs can lead by example and inspire their team members to do the same.

It is important for entrepreneurs to recognize that continuous learning and development is not a one-time event, but rather an ongoing process. As the business landscape continues to evolve, entrepreneurs must be willing to adapt and learn new skills in order to remain competitive. By embracing a mindset of continuous learning, entrepreneurs can position themselves and their businesses for long-term success.

In conclusion, continuous learning and development are crucial for entrepreneurs who want to thrive in today's dynamic business environment. By staying updated on industry trends, developing relevant skills, fostering a culture of learning, and investing in personal growth, entrepreneurs can enhance their ability to innovate and adapt to market changes. By embracing continuous learning, entrepreneurs can position themselves as leaders in their industry and drive long-term success for their businesses.

Section 8.4
Adapting to Market Changes

In today's fast-paced business environment, the ability to adapt to market changes is crucial for the long-term success of any entrepreneur. Markets are constantly evolving, driven by technological advancements, changing consumer preferences, and global economic shifts. To stay ahead of the competition and maintain a thriving business, entrepreneurs must be proactive in identifying and responding to these market changes.

One key aspect of adapting to market changes is staying informed and continuously monitoring industry trends. This involves keeping a close eye on market research, competitor analysis, and consumer behavior.

By staying up-to-date with the latest developments in the industry, entrepreneurs can identify emerging opportunities and potential threats. This knowledge allows them to make informed decisions and adjust their business strategies accordingly.

Adapting to market changes also requires a willingness to embrace innovation. Entrepreneurs should be open to exploring new technologies, processes, and business models that can help them stay relevant and competitive. This may involve investing in research and development, collaborating with industry experts, or seeking out partnerships with innovative startups. By embracing innovation, entrepreneurs can position themselves as leaders in their industry and attract customers who value forward-thinking solutions.

Flexibility is another crucial trait for adapting to market changes. Entrepreneurs must be willing to pivot their business strategies and adjust their offerings based on market demands. This may involve diversifying product lines, entering new markets, or even completely rebranding the business. By being flexible and responsive to market changes, entrepreneurs can ensure that their business remains relevant and meets the evolving needs of their target customers.

Adapting to market changes also requires a mindset of continuous learning and improvement. Entrepreneurs should actively seek feedback from customers, employees, and industry experts to identify areas for growth and refinement. This feedback can help entrepreneurs identify gaps in their offerings, improve customer satisfaction, and stay ahead of competitors. By constantly seeking ways to improve and adapt, entrepreneurs can position themselves as industry leaders and maintain a competitive edge.

Lastly, adapting to market changes requires a proactive approach to risk management. Entrepreneurs should anticipate potential risks and have contingency plans in place to mitigate their impact. This may involve diversifying revenue streams, building strong relationships with suppliers and partners, or investing in insurance and other risk management strategies. By being proactive in managing risks, entrepreneurs can navigate market changes with confidence and minimize potential disruptions to their business.

In conclusion, adapting to market changes is a critical skill for successful entrepreneurs. By staying informed, embracing innovation, being flexible, continuously learning, and managing risks, entrepreneurs can position themselves for long-term success in a rapidly evolving business landscape. By adapting to market changes, entrepreneurs can ensure that their business remains relevant, competitive, and resilient in the face of uncertainty.

Section 8.5
Anticipating Future Trends

Innovation and adaptation are crucial for the long-term success of any business. As an entrepreneur, it is essential to stay ahead of the curve and anticipate future trends in order to remain competitive in a rapidly changing market. By identifying and understanding emerging trends, you can position your business to take advantage of new opportunities and stay relevant to your customers.

One way to anticipate future trends is by closely monitoring industry developments and staying informed about the latest advancements in technology, consumer behavior, and market dynamics. This can be done through market research, attending industry conferences and events, and networking with other professionals in your field. By staying connected to the pulse of your industry, you can gain valuable insights into emerging trends and potential disruptions that may impact your business.

Another effective strategy for anticipating future trends is to analyze data and gather insights from your own business operations. By tracking key performance indicators, customer feedback, and market trends, you can identify patterns and make informed predictions about future developments. For example, if you notice a growing demand for eco-friendly products or a shift towards online shopping, you can proactively adapt your business model to meet these changing consumer preferences.

Additionally, it is important to pay attention to broader societal and global trends that may impact your industry. Factors such as demographic shifts, economic conditions, and regulatory changes can all influence consumer behavior and market dynamics. By staying informed about these external factors, you can anticipate how they may shape future trends and adjust your business strategies accordingly.

Innovation and adaptation go hand in hand when it comes to anticipating future trends. By fostering a culture of creativity and encouraging employees to think outside the box, you can generate new ideas and solutions that address emerging customer needs. This can involve investing in research and development, collaborating with external partners, or exploring new technologies and business models.

Furthermore, it is important to continuously evaluate and reassess your business strategies in light of changing trends. What may have worked in the past may not be effective in the future, so it is crucial to be flexible and willing to adapt. This may involve making strategic pivots, launching new products or services, or entering new markets.

In conclusion, anticipating future trends is a critical aspect of innovation and adaptation for entrepreneurs. By staying informed, analyzing data, and fostering a culture of creativity, you can position your business to thrive in a rapidly changing market. By proactively identifying and embracing emerging trends, you can stay ahead of the competition and ensure the long-term success of your business.

Section 8.6
Staying Ahead of the Competition

In today's fast-paced business landscape, staying ahead of the competition is crucial for the long-term success of any entrepreneur. As markets evolve and customer preferences change, it is essential to continuously innovate and adapt to maintain a competitive edge. In this section, we will explore strategies and techniques that successful entrepreneurs employ to stay ahead of their competitors.

One key aspect of staying ahead of the competition is to constantly monitor and analyze the market. By keeping a close eye on industry trends, emerging technologies, and customer demands, entrepreneurs can identify new opportunities and potential threats. This proactive approach allows them to make informed decisions and stay ahead of their competitors who may be slower to react.

Another important strategy is to foster a culture of innovation within the organization. Successful entrepreneurs encourage their teams to think creatively and challenge the status quo. They create an environment where new ideas are welcomed and experimentation is encouraged. By fostering a culture of innovation, entrepreneurs can continuously develop new products, services, and processes that differentiate them from their competitors.

Furthermore, successful entrepreneurs understand the importance of embracing technology and automation. They leverage the power of technology to streamline their operations, improve efficiency, and deliver better customer experiences. By adopting the latest tools and technologies, entrepreneurs can gain a competitive advantage and stay ahead of their competitors who may be slower to embrace change.

Continuous learning and development are also crucial for staying ahead of the competition. Successful entrepreneurs invest in their own personal growth and encourage their teams to do the same. They attend industry conferences, participate in workshops, and seek out new knowledge and skills. By staying up-to-date with the latest industry trends and best practices, entrepreneurs can adapt their strategies and stay ahead of their competitors.

In addition to continuous learning, successful entrepreneurs also prioritize networking and building relationships within their industry. They actively seek out opportunities to connect with other entrepreneurs, industry experts, and potential partners. By building a strong network, entrepreneurs can gain valuable insights, access new resources, and stay informed about industry developments. These connections can also lead to collaborations and partnerships that can give them a competitive advantage.

Lastly, staying ahead of the competition requires a mindset of constant improvement and a willingness to take calculated risks. Successful entrepreneurs are not afraid to challenge themselves and their businesses. They are open to feedback and are willing to pivot their strategies if necessary. By embracing change and taking calculated risks, entrepreneurs can adapt to market shifts and stay ahead of their competitors.

In conclusion, staying ahead of the competition is a continuous process that requires innovation, adaptation, and a proactive mindset. By monitoring the market, fostering a culture of innovation, embracing technology, continuous learning, networking, and taking calculated risks, entrepreneurs can position themselves as industry leaders and maintain a competitive edge. In the ever-evolving business landscape, staying ahead of the competition is not just a goal, but a necessity for long-term success.

Chapter 9
Effective Leadership and Team

Management

Section 9.1
Developing Leadership Skills

Developing strong leadership skills is crucial for entrepreneurs who want to effectively manage their teams and drive their businesses towards success. Leadership is not just about giving orders and making decisions; it is about inspiring and motivating others to achieve their full potential. In this section, we will explore some key strategies and techniques that can help entrepreneurs develop their leadership skills.

One important aspect of developing leadership skills is self-awareness. Effective leaders understand their strengths and weaknesses, and they continuously work on improving themselves. They seek feedback from their team members and actively listen to their concerns and suggestions. By being self-aware, leaders can identify areas for growth and take steps to develop the necessary skills.

Another important aspect of leadership is the ability to communicate effectively. Leaders must be able to clearly articulate their vision and goals to their team members. They should also be good listeners, open to feedback and ideas from others. Effective communication helps build trust and fosters a collaborative work environment.

Leadership also involves making tough decisions. Entrepreneurs need to be able to analyze situations, weigh the pros and cons, and make informed choices. They should be able to take risks and be comfortable with uncertainty. By making confident decisions, leaders inspire confidence in their team members and create a sense of direction.

Furthermore, leaders should be able to inspire and motivate their team members. They should lead by example and set high standards for themselves and their team. By demonstrating a strong work ethic and a positive attitude, leaders can inspire their team members to give their best effort. They should also provide regular feedback and recognition to acknowledge the achievements of their team members.

In addition to inspiring and motivating, leaders should also empower their team members. They should delegate tasks and responsibilities, giving their team members the opportunity to grow and develop their skills. By empowering others, leaders create a sense of ownership and accountability within the team.

Lastly, effective leaders are adaptable and open to change. They understand that the business landscape is constantly evolving, and they are willing to embrace new ideas and approaches. They encourage innovation and creativity within their team and are open to feedback and suggestions for improvement.

Developing leadership skills is an ongoing process. It requires self-reflection, continuous learning, and practice. By focusing on self-awareness, effective communication, decision-making, inspiration, empowerment, and adaptability, entrepreneurs can develop the leadership skills necessary to lead their teams and build successful businesses.

Section 9.2
Building a High-Performing Team

Building a high-performing team is crucial for the success of any business. As an entrepreneur, it is your responsibility to create an environment that fosters collaboration, innovation, and productivity. In this section, we will explore strategies and best practices for building a team that consistently delivers exceptional results.

One of the first steps in building a high-performing team is to clearly define the roles and responsibilities of each team member. This ensures that everyone understands their individual contributions and how they fit into the overall goals of the business. By setting clear expectations, you can minimize confusion and promote accountability within the team.

Another important aspect of building a high-performing team is hiring the right people. Look for individuals who not only have the necessary skills and experience but also align with the values and culture of your organization. A diverse team with a range of perspectives and backgrounds can bring fresh ideas and creativity to the table.

Once you have assembled your team, it is essential to

foster a positive work environment. Encourage open communication, collaboration, and mutual respect among team members. Create opportunities for team building activities and encourage social interactions outside of work. A supportive and inclusive work culture can significantly enhance team morale and productivity.

Effective leadership plays a crucial role in building a high-performing team. As a leader, it is important to lead by example and set high standards for performance. Provide regular feedback and recognition to motivate and inspire your team members. Encourage professional development and provide opportunities for growth within the organization. By investing in the growth and development of your team, you can create a sense of loyalty and commitment.

Building trust within the team is also essential for high performance. Trust is built through open and honest communication, transparency, and consistency. Encourage team members to share their ideas and opinions without fear of judgment or reprisal. Foster a culture of collaboration and encourage constructive feedback. When team members trust each other, they are more likely to take risks, share knowledge, and work together towards common goals.

In addition to building trust, it is important to empower your team members. Delegate responsibilities and give them the autonomy to make decisions within their areas of expertise. This not only helps to develop their skills and confidence but also fosters a sense of ownership and accountability. Empowered team members are more likely to take initiative, be proactive, and contribute to the overall success of the business.

Finally, building a high-performing team requires ongoing evaluation and improvement. Regularly assess the performance of your team members and provide constructive feedback. Identify areas for improvement and provide the necessary support and resources to help them succeed. Continuously invest in training and development opportunities to enhance the skills and capabilities of your team.

In conclusion, building a high-performing team is a critical aspect of effective leadership and team management. By clearly defining roles, hiring the right people, fostering a positive work environment, providing effective leadership, building trust, empowering team members, and continuously evaluating and improving, you can create a team that consistently delivers exceptional results. Remember, a high-performing team is not just a group of individuals working together, but a cohesive unit that shares a common vision and works towards a shared goal.

Section 9.3
Effective Communication and Collaboration

Effective communication and collaboration are essential skills for successful leaders and team managers. In order to achieve organizational goals and foster a positive work environment, leaders must be able to effectively communicate their vision, expectations, and feedback to their team members. Additionally, they must encourage open and transparent communication among team members to promote collaboration and innovation. One key aspect of effective communication is active listening. Leaders should actively listen to their team members, giving them their full attention and showing genuine interest in what they have to say. This not only helps build trust and rapport but also allows leaders to gain valuable insights and perspectives from their team members. By actively listening, leaders can better understand the needs, concerns, and ideas of their team, leading to more effective decision-making and problem-solving.

Another important aspect of effective communication is clarity. Leaders should strive to communicate their expectations and goals clearly and concisely, ensuring that their team members understand what is expected of them. This includes providing clear instructions, setting realistic deadlines, and providing regular feedback and updates. Clear communication helps avoid misunderstandings and ensures that everyone is on the same page, working towards a common goal.

In addition to effective communication, collaboration is crucial for team success. Leaders should create an environment that encourages collaboration and teamwork, where team members feel comfortable sharing ideas, asking for help, and working together towards a shared objective. This can be achieved through team-building activities, fostering a culture of trust and respect, and providing opportunities for cross-functional collaboration.

Collaboration also involves effective delegation. Leaders should delegate tasks and responsibilities to team members based on their strengths and expertise, empowering them to take ownership and contribute to the team's success. By delegating effectively, leaders not only lighten their own workload but also foster a sense of trust and empowerment among team members. Furthermore, effective communication and collaboration require the use of appropriate communication channels and tools. Leaders should leverage technology and digital platforms to facilitate communication and collaboration, especially in remote or distributed teams. This includes using project management software, video conferencing tools, and instant messaging platforms to ensure seamless communication and collaboration across different locations and time zones.

Lastly, leaders should lead by example when it comes to effective communication and collaboration. They should demonstrate active listening, clear communication, and collaboration in their own interactions with team members. By modeling these behaviors, leaders set the tone for the entire team and create a culture of effective communication and collaboration.

In conclusion, effective communication and

collaboration are essential for effective leadership and team management. By actively listening, communicating clearly, fostering collaboration, and leading by example, leaders can create a positive work environment and drive team success. These skills are crucial for building strong relationships, promoting innovation, and achieving organizational goals.

Section 9.4
Motivating and Inspiring Employees

Motivating and inspiring employees is a crucial aspect of effective leadership and team management. When employees feel motivated and inspired, they are more likely to be engaged, productive, and committed to the success of the business. As a leader, it is your responsibility to create an environment that fosters motivation and inspiration among your team members.

One of the key ways to motivate and inspire employees is by setting clear goals and expectations. When employees have a clear understanding of what is expected of them and what they are working towards, they are more likely to feel motivated to achieve those goals. It is important to communicate these goals effectively and provide regular feedback and recognition for their efforts.

Another important factor in motivating and inspiring employees is creating a positive work culture. This includes fostering a supportive and inclusive environment where employees feel valued and appreciated. Encouraging teamwork, collaboration, and open communication can also contribute to a positive work culture. When employees feel that their opinions and ideas are valued, they are more likely to be motivated to contribute their best work.

Providing opportunities for growth and development is another effective way to motivate and inspire employees. This can include offering training programs, mentorship opportunities, and career advancement prospects. When employees see that there are opportunities for them to learn and grow within the organization, they are more likely to be motivated to perform at their best.

Recognition and rewards are also powerful motivators. Acknowledging and appreciating the efforts and achievements of employees can go a long way in boosting their motivation and inspiring them to continue performing well. This can be done through verbal praise, written recognition, or even tangible rewards such as bonuses or promotions.

In addition to these strategies, it is important for leaders to lead by example. When leaders demonstrate passion, enthusiasm, and a strong work ethic, it can inspire employees to do the same. Being transparent and honest in your communication, and showing empathy and understanding towards your team members, can also contribute to a positive and motivating work environment.

Overall, motivating and inspiring employees requires a combination of clear communication, a positive work culture, opportunities for growth, recognition and rewards, and leading by example. By implementing these strategies, leaders can create a motivated and inspired team that is committed to the success of the business.

Section 9.5
Delegating and Empowering Others

Delegating and empowering others is a crucial aspect of effective leadership and team management. As an entrepreneur, it is important to recognize that you cannot do everything on your own. Delegation involves assigning tasks and responsibilities to team members who have the skills and capabilities to handle them. By delegating, you not only lighten your workload but also provide opportunities for growth and development within your team.

When delegating tasks, it is essential to clearly communicate your expectations and objectives. Ensure that the team member understands the desired outcome and any specific guidelines or deadlines. This clarity will help them take ownership of the task and work towards achieving the desired results. Additionally, provide any necessary resources or support to enable them to complete the task successfully.

Empowering others goes hand in hand with delegation. It involves giving team members the authority and autonomy to make decisions and take action. By empowering your team, you foster a sense of trust and confidence, which can lead to increased motivation and productivity. When team members feel empowered, they are more likely to take initiative, think creatively, and contribute their unique perspectives to problem-solving.

To effectively empower others, it is important to create a supportive and inclusive work environment. Encourage open communication and collaboration, where team members feel comfortable sharing their ideas and opinions. Provide opportunities for skill development and training, allowing team members to enhance their capabilities and take on more challenging tasks. Recognize and celebrate their achievements, reinforcing their sense of value and contribution to the team's success.

However, it is crucial to strike a balance between delegation and empowerment. While it is important to trust your team members and give them autonomy, it is equally important to provide guidance and support when needed. Regularly check in with your team members to provide feedback, offer guidance, and address any challenges they may be facing. This ongoing communication ensures that everyone is aligned and working towards the same goals.

Delegating and empowering others not only benefits your team but also allows you to focus on strategic decision-making and higher-level tasks. It enables you to leverage the diverse skills and expertise within your team, leading to increased efficiency and productivity. By empowering your team members, you create a culture of trust, collaboration, and continuous improvement, which is essential for long-term success and growth.

In conclusion, effective leadership and team management involve delegating tasks and empowering others. By delegating, you distribute workload and provide growth opportunities for your team members. Empowering others fosters trust, motivation, and creativity within the team. Striking a balance between delegation and empowerment is crucial, and regular communication and support are essential for success. By delegating and empowering, you create a strong and capable team that can contribute to the overall success of your business.

Section 9.6
Resolving Conflicts and Managing Challenges

Conflict is an inevitable part of any team or organization. As a leader, it is crucial to have the skills and strategies to effectively resolve conflicts and manage challenges that arise within your team. Conflict can arise from differences in opinions, goals, or personalities, and if left unaddressed, it can lead to a toxic work environment and hinder productivity.

One of the first steps in resolving conflicts is to acknowledge and address them promptly. Ignoring conflicts or hoping they will resolve themselves often leads to escalation and further damage to relationships. As a leader, it is important to create an open and safe space for team members to express their concerns and grievances.

Active listening is a key skill in conflict resolution. It involves giving your full attention to the person speaking, without interrupting or judging. By actively listening, you can gain a better understanding of the underlying issues and emotions involved in the conflict. This understanding will help you find a resolution that addresses the root cause of the conflict rather than just the surface-level disagreement.

Once you have listened to all parties involved, it is important to facilitate a constructive dialogue.

Encourage team members to express their perspectives and concerns while maintaining a respectful and professional tone. As a leader, you should act as a mediator, guiding the conversation and ensuring that everyone has an opportunity to be heard.

In some cases, conflicts may require a compromise or finding a middle ground that satisfies all parties involved. However, it is important to note that not all conflicts can be resolved through compromise. In such cases, it may be necessary to make a difficult decision or seek outside help, such as involving a neutral third party or a professional mediator.

Managing challenges goes hand in hand with resolving conflicts. Challenges can arise from various sources, such as changes in the market, technological advancements, or internal issues within the team. As a leader, it is important to anticipate and proactively address these challenges to minimize their impact on the team and the business.

When faced with challenges, it is important to remain calm and composed. Panicking or reacting impulsively can lead to poor decision-making and further exacerbate the situation. Instead, take a step back, assess the situation objectively, and gather all the necessary information before formulating a plan of action.

Effective communication is crucial when managing challenges. Keep your team informed about the situation, the potential impact, and the steps being taken to address it. Transparency and open communication build trust and confidence within the team, fostering a sense of unity and collaboration.

In addition to communication, it is important to leverage the strengths and expertise of your team members when facing challenges. Encourage collaboration and brainstorming sessions to generate innovative solutions. By involving your team in the problem-solving process, you not only tap into their collective knowledge but also empower them to take ownership of the challenges and contribute to their resolution.

Lastly, it is important to learn from challenges and conflicts. Take the time to reflect on what went wrong and identify areas for improvement. Use these experiences as opportunities for growth and development, both for yourself as a leader and for your team as a whole. By continuously learning and adapting, you can build a resilient and high-performing team that is capable of overcoming any challenge that comes their way.

In conclusion, resolving conflicts and managing challenges is an essential aspect of effective leadership and team management. By addressing conflicts promptly, actively listening, facilitating constructive dialogue, and making difficult decisions when necessary, leaders can create a positive and productive work environment. Similarly, by remaining calm, communicating effectively, leveraging the strengths of the team, and learning from challenges, leaders can navigate through obstacles and foster a culture of continuous improvement and success.

Chapter 10
Building a Strong Company Culture

Section 10.1
Defining Core Values and Mission

Defining core values and mission is a crucial step in building a strong company culture. Core values are the fundamental beliefs and principles that guide the behavior and decision-making of an organization. They serve as a compass, providing a clear direction for the company and its employees. Mission, on the other hand, is the purpose or reason for the existence of the company. It defines what the company aims to achieve and the impact it wants to make in the world.

When defining core values, it is important to involve key stakeholders, including employees, in the process. This ensures that the values are representative of the entire organization and not just a top-down imposition. Core values should reflect the company's identity, culture, and aspirations. They should be authentic and resonate with both employees and customers.

To define core values, start by identifying the qualities and behaviors that are important to the company. Consider what sets the company apart from its competitors and what values are essential for success. These values can include integrity, innovation, teamwork, customer focus, accountability, and more. It is important to keep the list of core values concise, typically no more than five or six, to ensure clarity and focus.

Once the core values are defined, it is crucial to communicate them effectively to all employees. This can be done through internal communications, such as company-wide meetings, newsletters, and intranet platforms. It is also important to integrate the core values into various aspects of the company, including hiring processes, performance evaluations, and recognition programs. By consistently reinforcing the core values, they become ingrained in the company culture and guide the behavior of employees at all levels. In addition to core values, defining a clear mission is essential for building a strong company culture. The mission statement should articulate the company's purpose, its target audience, and the value it aims to deliver. A well-crafted mission statement inspires employees and aligns their efforts towards a common goal. It also helps attract customers who resonate with the company's mission and values.

When defining the mission, it is important to consider the company's long-term vision and strategic goals. The mission should be ambitious yet realistic, providing a sense of purpose and direction. It should also be specific and concise, making it easy for employees and customers to understand and remember.

Once the core values and mission are defined, it is important to regularly revisit and evaluate them. As the company evolves and grows, the core values and mission may need to be adjusted to reflect changing circumstances. It is also important to ensure that the core values and mission are not just empty words, but are actively lived and demonstrated by leaders and employees.

In conclusion, defining core values and mission is a critical step in building a strong company culture. Core values provide a guiding compass for the behavior and decision-making of the organization, while the mission statement articulates the company's purpose and value proposition. By involving key stakeholders in the process, communicating the core values effectively, and regularly evaluating and living them, companies can create a culture that attracts and retains top talent, inspires employees, and drives long-term success.

Section 10.2

Fostering a Positive Work Environment

Creating a positive work environment is crucial for the success and growth of any business. When employees feel valued, supported, and motivated, they are more likely to be engaged, productive, and committed to their work. Fostering a positive work environment involves creating a culture that promotes collaboration, open communication, and a sense of belonging.

One of the key aspects of fostering a positive work environment is promoting a culture of respect and inclusivity. This means treating all employees with fairness, dignity, and equality, regardless of their background, gender, race, or any other characteristic. Encouraging diversity and inclusion not only helps to create a more harmonious workplace, but it also brings different perspectives and ideas to the table, leading to innovation and better decision-making.

Another important factor in fostering a positive work environment is providing opportunities for growth and development. Employees want to feel that their work is meaningful and that they have the chance to learn and advance in their careers. Offering training programs, mentorship opportunities, and clear career paths can help employees feel valued and motivated to contribute their best.

Communication is also key in creating a positive work environment. Open and transparent communication channels allow employees to express their ideas, concerns, and feedback freely. Regular team meetings, one-on-one check-ins, and anonymous suggestion boxes can all contribute to a culture of open communication. Additionally, providing timely and constructive feedback helps employees understand their strengths and areas for improvement, fostering a culture of continuous learning and growth.

Recognition and appreciation are powerful tools for fostering a positive work environment. Acknowledging and celebrating employees' achievements and milestones not only boosts morale but also reinforces a culture of recognition and appreciation. This can be done through formal recognition programs, such as employee of the month awards, as well as informal gestures, such as a simple thank you or a note of appreciation.

Creating a positive work environment also involves promoting work-life balance. Encouraging employees to take breaks, providing flexible work arrangements, and offering wellness programs can help reduce stress and promote overall well-being. When employees feel supported in achieving a healthy work-life balance, they are more likely to be engaged and productive.

Lastly, fostering a positive work environment requires leadership commitment and role modeling. Leaders should embody the values and behaviors they want to see in their employees. By demonstrating respect, inclusivity, and open communication, leaders set the tone for the entire organization. They should also actively listen to their employees, address concerns, and take action to create a supportive and positive work environment.

In conclusion, fostering a positive work environment is essential for building a strong company culture. By promoting respect, inclusivity, growth opportunities, open communication, recognition, work-life balance, and leadership commitment, businesses can create an environment where employees thrive, leading to increased productivity, employee satisfaction, and overall success.

Section 10.3

Encouraging Diversity and Inclusion

In today's rapidly evolving business landscape, diversity and inclusion have become crucial elements of building a strong company culture. Embracing diversity means recognizing and valuing the unique perspectives, backgrounds, and experiences that individuals bring to the table. Inclusion, on the other hand, involves creating an environment where everyone feels welcome, respected, and empowered to contribute their best.

Encouraging diversity and inclusion within your organization can have numerous benefits. Firstly, it fosters innovation and creativity by bringing together individuals with different viewpoints and ideas. When people from diverse backgrounds collaborate, they can offer fresh insights and approaches that can lead to breakthrough solutions and competitive advantages.

Moreover, a diverse and inclusive workplace can enhance employee engagement and satisfaction. When employees feel valued and included, they are more likely to be motivated, productive, and committed to the organization's goals. This, in turn, can lead to higher retention rates and attract top talent who are seeking an inclusive work environment.

To encourage diversity and inclusion, it is essential to establish policies and practices that promote equal opportunities for all employees. This includes implementing fair hiring and promotion processes that focus on merit rather than biases. It is crucial to create a diverse candidate pool and ensure that the selection process is free from discrimination.

Additionally, providing diversity and inclusion training for employees can help raise awareness and foster a culture of respect and understanding. This training should address unconscious biases, stereotypes, and microaggressions, and provide strategies for creating an inclusive work environment.

Leadership plays a vital role in encouraging diversity and inclusion. Leaders should set the tone by actively promoting and championing diversity initiatives. They should lead by example, demonstrating inclusive behaviors and creating opportunities for diverse voices to be heard. By fostering an inclusive culture, leaders can inspire others to embrace diversity and contribute to a more inclusive workplace.

Creating employee resource groups or affinity networks can also be an effective way to encourage diversity and inclusion. These groups provide a platform for employees with shared backgrounds or interests to connect, support one another, and advocate for change within the organization. They can help foster a sense of belonging and provide opportunities for networking and professional development.

Furthermore, it is important to regularly assess and measure the progress of diversity and inclusion initiatives. This can be done through employee surveys, focus groups, or diversity metrics. By tracking progress, organizations can identify areas for improvement and make necessary adjustments to ensure ongoing commitment to diversity and inclusion.

In conclusion, encouraging diversity and inclusion is essential for building a strong company culture. By embracing diversity, organizations can tap into the power of different perspectives and experiences, leading to innovation and improved business outcomes. Creating an inclusive work environment where everyone feels valued and empowered fosters employee engagement and satisfaction. Through leadership, training, and the establishment of inclusive policies and practices, organizations can create a culture that celebrates diversity and promotes equal opportunities for all.

Section 10.4
Recognizing and Rewarding Success

Recognizing and rewarding success is a crucial aspect of building a strong company culture. When employees feel valued and appreciated for their hard work and achievements, it not only boosts their morale but also motivates them to continue performing at their best. In this section, we will explore the importance of recognizing and rewarding success and discuss various strategies that can be implemented to create a culture of appreciation within your organization.

One of the most effective ways to recognize and reward success is through regular and timely feedback. Providing constructive feedback to employees allows them to understand their strengths and areas for improvement. It is important to acknowledge and celebrate their accomplishments, whether big or small, as it reinforces positive behavior and encourages a sense of pride in their work.

In addition to feedback, implementing a formal recognition program can be highly beneficial. This can include employee of the month awards, quarterly or annual recognition ceremonies, or even a peer-to-peer recognition system. By publicly acknowledging and appreciating the efforts of individuals or teams, you create a culture that values and celebrates success.

Another way to recognize and reward success is through incentives and rewards. This can be in the form of monetary bonuses, gift cards, or even extra time off. By offering tangible rewards, you not only show appreciation for their hard work but also provide an incentive for others to strive for excellence.

It is also important to create a culture of continuous learning and development. Providing opportunities for employees to enhance their skills and knowledge not only benefits them individually but also contributes to the overall success of the organization. Recognizing and rewarding employees who actively seek out learning opportunities and demonstrate a commitment to personal growth can further encourage a culture of continuous improvement.

Furthermore, fostering a supportive and collaborative work environment can greatly contribute to recognizing and rewarding success. Encouraging teamwork and collaboration allows employees to feel valued for their contributions and creates a sense of camaraderie within the organization. Recognizing and rewarding successful team efforts can further strengthen the bonds between team members and promote a culture of shared success.

Lastly, it is important to remember that recognition and rewards should be tailored to individual preferences and needs. Some employees may prefer public recognition, while others may appreciate a more private acknowledgment. Taking the time to understand and cater to individual preferences ensures that the recognition and rewards are meaningful and impactful.

In conclusion, recognizing and rewarding success is a vital component of building a strong company culture. By providing regular feedback, implementing formal recognition programs, offering incentives and rewards, fostering a culture of continuous learning, promoting collaboration, and tailoring recognition to individual preferences, you can create an environment where employees feel valued and motivated to achieve their best. This not only contributes to the overall success of the organization but also enhances employee satisfaction and engagement.

Section 10.5
Promoting Work-Life Balance

In today's fast-paced and demanding business world, promoting work-life balance has become increasingly important for entrepreneurs and their employees. A strong company culture that values the well-being and happiness of its workforce can lead to increased productivity, employee satisfaction, and overall success. Promoting work-life balance starts with creating a supportive and flexible work environment. Entrepreneurs should encourage their employees to prioritize their personal lives and take time for themselves outside of work. This can be achieved by offering flexible work hours, remote work options, and paid time off policies that allow for vacations and personal days.

Additionally, entrepreneurs should lead by example and demonstrate the importance of work-life balance in their own lives. By setting boundaries and taking time for self-care, entrepreneurs can show their employees that it is possible to achieve success without sacrificing personal well-being.

Another way to promote work-life balance is by fostering a culture of open communication and trust within the company. Entrepreneurs should encourage their employees to speak up if they are feeling overwhelmed or burnt out. By providing support and resources, such as employee assistance programs or wellness initiatives, entrepreneurs can help their employees manage stress and maintain a healthy work-life balance.

Furthermore, entrepreneurs can promote work-life balance by encouraging their employees to disconnect from work outside of office hours. This can be achieved by implementing policies that discourage after-hours emails or phone calls, and by encouraging employees to take breaks and vacations without feeling guilty or pressured.

Promoting work-life balance also involves recognizing and celebrating achievements both inside and outside of the workplace. Entrepreneurs should acknowledge and reward their employees for their hard work and accomplishments, while also celebrating personal milestones and achievements. This can help create a positive and supportive work environment where employees feel valued and appreciated.

In conclusion, promoting work-life balance is essential for building a strong company culture. By creating a supportive and flexible work environment, fostering open communication and trust, encouraging employees to disconnect from work outside of office hours, and recognizing achievements both inside and outside of the workplace, entrepreneurs can create a culture that values the well-being and happiness of their workforce. Ultimately, this can lead to increased productivity, employee satisfaction, and long-term success for the business.

Section 10.6
Creating a Culture of Continuous Improvement

Creating a culture of continuous improvement is essential for the long-term success and sustainability of any business. It involves fostering an environment where employees are encouraged to constantly seek ways to enhance their skills, processes, and overall performance. By embracing a mindset of continuous improvement, companies can stay ahead of the competition, adapt to changing market dynamics, and drive innovation.

One of the key aspects of creating a culture of continuous improvement is promoting a learning mindset among employees. This involves encouraging them to actively seek out opportunities for growth and development, both personally and professionally. Providing access to training programs, workshops, and educational resources can help employees acquire new knowledge and skills that can be applied to their work.

In addition to promoting a learning mindset, it is important to establish a feedback-driven culture within the organization. Regular feedback sessions, performance evaluations, and open communication channels can enable employees to receive constructive criticism and suggestions for improvement. This feedback should be focused on specific areas where individuals can enhance their performance and contribute to the overall success of the company.

Another crucial element of creating a culture of continuous improvement is empowering employees to take ownership of their work and contribute their ideas.

Encouraging a sense of ownership and autonomy can motivate employees to proactively identify areas for improvement and propose innovative solutions. This can be achieved through initiatives such as suggestion boxes, brainstorming sessions, and cross-functional collaboration.

Furthermore, it is important to recognize and celebrate the efforts and achievements of employees who actively contribute to the culture of continuous improvement. This can be done through rewards, incentives, and public recognition. By acknowledging and appreciating the dedication and commitment of individuals who strive for excellence, companies can reinforce the importance of continuous improvement and inspire others to follow suit.

To sustain a culture of continuous improvement, it is crucial for leaders and managers to lead by example. They should demonstrate a commitment to their own personal growth and development, as well as actively support and encourage the growth of their team members. By embodying the values and behaviors associated with continuous improvement, leaders can inspire and motivate their employees to embrace the same mindset.

In conclusion, creating a culture of continuous improvement is vital for building a strong company culture. By promoting a learning mindset, fostering a feedback-driven culture, empowering employees, recognizing achievements, and leading by example, businesses can cultivate an environment where continuous improvement becomes ingrained in the company's DNA. This culture of continuous improvement not only enhances individual and team performance but also drives innovation, adaptability, and long-term success.

Chapter 11
Long-Term Sustainability and Success

Section 11.1
Strategic Planning for the Future

Strategic planning is a crucial aspect of ensuring long-term sustainability and success for any business. It involves setting clear goals and objectives, identifying potential challenges and opportunities, and developing a roadmap to guide the organization towards its desired future state.

One of the key elements of strategic planning is conducting a thorough analysis of the business environment. This includes assessing market trends, competitor activities, and customer preferences. By understanding the external factors that can impact the business, entrepreneurs can make informed decisions and adapt their strategies accordingly.

Another important aspect of strategic planning is defining the company's vision and mission. This provides a sense of purpose and direction, guiding decision-making and resource allocation. A well-defined vision and mission statement also helps in aligning the entire organization towards a common goal, fostering a sense of unity and motivation among employees.

In addition to setting goals and defining a vision, strategic planning involves developing actionable strategies and initiatives. These strategies should be based on a thorough understanding of the business's strengths, weaknesses, opportunities, and threats. By leveraging strengths and addressing weaknesses, entrepreneurs can position their businesses for long-term success.

Furthermore, strategic planning should also consider potential risks and uncertainties. This includes identifying potential threats to the business, such as changes in regulations or shifts in consumer behavior. By proactively addressing these risks and developing contingency plans, entrepreneurs can mitigate potential disruptions and ensure the sustainability of their businesses.

It is important to note that strategic planning is not a one-time activity. It should be an ongoing process that is regularly reviewed and updated. As the business landscape evolves, entrepreneurs need to adapt their strategies to stay relevant and competitive. This requires continuous monitoring of market trends, competitor activities, and customer feedback.

In conclusion, strategic planning is a critical component of long-term sustainability and success for entrepreneurs. By setting clear goals, defining a vision, and developing actionable strategies, entrepreneurs can navigate the ever-changing business landscape and position their businesses for growth and prosperity.

Regular review and adaptation of strategies are essential to ensure continued success in the future

Section 11.2
Managing Risks and Uncertainties

In order to ensure long-term sustainability and success, entrepreneurs must be adept at managing risks and uncertainties. Running a business inherently involves taking risks, but it is crucial to have strategies in place to mitigate potential negative outcomes and navigate uncertain situations.

One key aspect of managing risks is conducting a thorough risk assessment. This involves identifying and analyzing potential risks that could impact the business, such as economic downturns, changes in regulations, or technological disruptions. By understanding these risks, entrepreneurs can develop contingency plans and implement measures to minimize their impact.

Another important aspect of risk management is diversification. By diversifying their business offerings, entrepreneurs can spread their risks across different products or services, markets, or customer segments. This can help protect the business from being overly reliant on a single source of revenue and reduce the impact of any potential disruptions.

Entrepreneurs should also consider the importance of insurance in managing risks. Having appropriate insurance coverage can provide financial protection in the event of unforeseen circumstances, such as natural disasters, accidents, or legal liabilities. It is essential to regularly review and update insurance policies to ensure they adequately cover the business's evolving needs.

Furthermore, staying informed and keeping up with industry trends and market changes is crucial for managing risks and uncertainties. By staying ahead of the curve, entrepreneurs can anticipate potential challenges and adapt their strategies accordingly. This may involve monitoring competitors, conducting market research, and staying informed about technological advancements that could impact the industry.

Effective communication and collaboration within the organization are also vital for managing risks. Entrepreneurs should foster a culture of open communication, where employees feel comfortable reporting potential risks or uncertainties. Regular meetings and discussions can help identify and address emerging risks in a timely manner.

Additionally, having a strong network of advisors and mentors can provide valuable insights and guidance in managing risks. Seeking advice from experienced professionals or joining industry associations can help entrepreneurs gain access to resources and expertise that can assist in risk management.

Lastly, it is important for entrepreneurs to maintain a positive mindset and embrace uncertainty as an opportunity for growth. While risks and uncertainties can be daunting, they also present opportunities for innovation and adaptation. By approaching challenges with a proactive and optimistic mindset, entrepreneurs can navigate uncertainties and position their businesses for long-term sustainability and success.

In conclusion, managing risks and uncertainties is a critical aspect of ensuring long-term sustainability and success for entrepreneurs. By conducting thorough risk assessments, diversifying business offerings, having appropriate insurance coverage, staying informed about industry trends, fostering effective communication, seeking advice from mentors, and maintaining a positive mindset, entrepreneurs can navigate uncertainties and position their businesses for growth and resilience.

Section 11.3
Building Strong Relationships with Stakeholders

Building strong relationships with stakeholders is crucial for the long-term sustainability and success of any business. Stakeholders are individuals or groups who have a vested interest in the company and can significantly impact its operations and outcomes. These stakeholders can include employees, customers, suppliers, investors, government agencies, and the local community.

One of the key aspects of building strong relationships with stakeholders is effective communication. Open and transparent communication helps to establish trust and understanding between the business and its stakeholders. Regularly updating stakeholders on the company's progress, challenges, and future plans can help to foster a sense of involvement and ownership.

Another important factor in building strong relationships with stakeholders is actively listening to their needs and concerns. By understanding their perspectives and addressing their issues, businesses can demonstrate their commitment to meeting stakeholder expectations. This can be achieved through surveys, feedback sessions, and regular meetings to gather input and feedback from stakeholders.

In addition to communication and listening, businesses should also prioritize delivering value to their stakeholders. This means understanding their needs and finding ways to meet or exceed their expectations. By consistently delivering high-quality products or services, providing excellent customer service, and maintaining fair and ethical business practices, businesses can build trust and loyalty among their stakeholders.

Collaboration is another key element in building strong relationships with stakeholders. By involving stakeholders in decision-making processes and seeking their input, businesses can create a sense of ownership and shared responsibility. This can lead to more effective problem-solving, innovation, and ultimately, better outcomes for all parties involved.

Furthermore, businesses should also consider the impact of their operations on the local community and the environment. Engaging in corporate social responsibility initiatives, such as supporting local charities, reducing environmental footprint, and promoting sustainable practices, can help to build positive relationships with stakeholders and enhance the company's reputation.

Lastly, it is important for businesses to regularly evaluate and reassess their relationships with stakeholders. This involves monitoring and measuring stakeholder satisfaction, identifying areas for improvement, and taking corrective actions when necessary. By continuously striving to strengthen relationships with stakeholders, businesses can ensure their long-term sustainability and success.

In conclusion, building strong relationships with stakeholders is essential for the long-term sustainability and success of a business. Effective communication, active listening, delivering value, collaboration, and corporate social responsibility are key strategies for fostering positive relationships with stakeholders. By prioritizing these efforts and continuously evaluating and improving relationships, businesses can create a supportive and mutually beneficial environment that contributes to their overall success.

Section 11.4
Corporate Social Responsibility

Corporate social responsibility (CSR) is a vital aspect of long-term sustainability and success for any business. It refers to the ethical and responsible actions that a company takes to contribute positively to society and the environment. In today's world, consumers and stakeholders are increasingly conscious of the impact businesses have on the world, and they expect companies to go beyond profit-making and actively engage in CSR initiatives.

One of the key benefits of practicing corporate social responsibility is the positive impact it has on a company's reputation. When a business demonstrates a genuine commitment to social and environmental issues, it builds trust and credibility with its customers, employees, and the wider community. This can lead to increased customer loyalty, improved employee morale, and a stronger brand image, ultimately contributing to long-term success.

There are various ways in which businesses can engage in corporate social responsibility. One common approach is through philanthropy and charitable giving. This involves donating a portion of profits or resources to support causes and organizations that align with the company's values and mission. By investing in initiatives such as education, healthcare, or environmental conservation, businesses can make a tangible difference in the communities they operate in.

Another important aspect of CSR is adopting sustainable business practices. This includes reducing the company's carbon footprint, conserving resources, and minimizing waste and pollution. By implementing environmentally friendly practices, businesses not only contribute to a healthier planet but also often realize cost savings through improved efficiency and resource management.

Furthermore, corporate social responsibility involves treating employees fairly and ethically. This includes providing a safe and inclusive work environment, offering competitive wages and benefits, and promoting diversity and equal opportunities. By prioritizing the well-being and development of their employees, businesses can foster a positive company culture and attract top talent, leading to increased productivity and long-term success.

Engaging in CSR also extends to responsible supply chain management. Businesses should ensure that their suppliers and partners adhere to ethical and sustainable practices. This includes fair labor conditions, responsible sourcing of materials, and compliance with human rights standards. By holding their supply chain accountable, businesses can mitigate risks and ensure that their operations align with their CSR commitments.

In conclusion, corporate social responsibility is not just a moral obligation but also a strategic business practice. By actively engaging in CSR initiatives, businesses can enhance their reputation, build stronger relationships with stakeholders, and contribute to a more sustainable and equitable world. Incorporating CSR into long-term sustainability and success strategies is essential for businesses that aim to thrive in today's socially conscious marketplace.

Section 11.5
Maintaining Ethical Business Practices

In today's business landscape, maintaining ethical practices is not only a moral obligation but also a crucial factor for long-term sustainability and success. Ethical business practices involve conducting business in a manner that is fair, transparent, and responsible towards all stakeholders, including customers, employees, suppliers, and the community at large.

One of the key aspects of maintaining ethical business

practices is ensuring honesty and integrity in all business dealings. This means being truthful and transparent in communication, delivering on promises, and upholding high ethical standards in all interactions. By doing so, entrepreneurs can build trust and credibility with their stakeholders, which is essential for long-term success.

Another important aspect of ethical business practices is treating employees with respect and fairness. This includes providing a safe and inclusive work environment, offering fair compensation and benefits, and promoting equal opportunities for growth and development. By valuing and respecting their employees, entrepreneurs can foster a positive work culture and enhance employee loyalty and productivity.

Furthermore, ethical business practices also involve being socially responsible and environmentally conscious. This means taking steps to minimize the negative impact of business operations on the environment, such as reducing waste, conserving energy, and adopting sustainable practices. Additionally, entrepreneurs can contribute to the well-being of the community by supporting local initiatives, engaging in philanthropy, and giving back to society.

In order to maintain ethical business practices, it is important for entrepreneurs to establish clear ethical guidelines and policies within their organizations. These guidelines should outline the expected behavior and conduct of employees, as well as the consequences for non-compliance. Regular training and communication about ethical practices can also help reinforce the importance of ethical behavior and ensure that all employees are aware of their responsibilities.

Moreover, entrepreneurs should also regularly assess and monitor their business practices to identify any potential ethical issues or conflicts of interest. This can be done through internal audits, feedback from stakeholders, and engagement with industry standards and regulations. By proactively addressing and resolving ethical concerns, entrepreneurs can demonstrate their commitment to ethical business practices and maintain the trust of their stakeholders.

In conclusion, maintaining ethical business practices is not only a moral imperative but also a strategic advantage for entrepreneurs. By conducting business in an ethical and responsible manner, entrepreneurs can build trust, enhance their reputation, and ensure long-term sustainability and success. By treating employees, customers, and the community with fairness and respect, entrepreneurs can create a positive work culture and contribute to the well-being of society. Ultimately, ethical business practices are not just a choice, but a fundamental requirement for building a thriving and sustainable business.

Section 11.6
Celebrating Milestones and Achievements

As entrepreneurs, it is important to recognize and celebrate the milestones and achievements that we reach along our journey towards long-term sustainability and success. These milestones serve as markers of progress and can provide a sense of accomplishment and motivation for both ourselves and our team.

Celebrating milestones and achievements not only

boosts morale and motivation, but it also fosters a positive and supportive work environment. When we take the time to acknowledge and appreciate the hard work and dedication that went into reaching a milestone or achieving a goal, it creates a sense of camaraderie and unity within the team.

One way to celebrate milestones and achievements is through recognition and rewards. This can be as simple as publicly acknowledging and thanking individuals or teams for their contributions during a team meeting or through a company-wide email. Recognizing the efforts and successes of others not only makes them feel valued and appreciated, but it also inspires others to strive for excellence.

In addition to recognition, rewards can also be given to celebrate milestones and achievements. These rewards can range from small tokens of appreciation, such as gift cards or personalized notes, to more significant rewards like bonuses or promotions. The key is to tailor the rewards to the significance of the milestone or achievement, ensuring that they are meaningful and impactful.

Another way to celebrate milestones and achievements

is through special events or activities. This can include team outings, parties, or even a company-wide celebration. These events provide an opportunity for the entire team to come together and celebrate their collective successes. It also allows for a moment of reflection and gratitude, as we recognize the progress we have made and the challenges we have overcome.

Celebrating milestones and achievements should not be limited to the big wins or major milestones. It is equally important to celebrate the small victories and incremental progress that we make along the way. By acknowledging and celebrating even the smallest achievements, we create a culture of continuous improvement and growth.

In conclusion, celebrating milestones and achievements is an essential part of building a strong and sustainable business. It boosts morale, fosters a positive work environment, and inspires continued success. Whether through recognition and rewards or special events and activities, taking the time to celebrate our accomplishments is a powerful way to motivate ourselves and our team on the path to long-term sustainability and success.

SUMMARY

"The Secrets of Successful Entrepreneurs: Strategies for Building a Thriving Business"is a comprehensive guide that equips aspiring entrepreneurs with the knowledge and tools needed to navigate the challenging world of business. From developing a growth mindset and identifying profitable opportunities to creating a solid business plan and implementing effective marketing strategies, this book covers all aspects of building a successful venture. It delves into the importance of sales and customer acquisition, financial management and planning, scaling and growth strategies, innovation and adaptation, effective leadership and team management, and building a strong company culture. With practical insights and actionable advice, this book empowers entrepreneurs to overcome obstacles, make informed decisions, and ultimately achieve long-term sustainability and success in their business endeavors.

www.ingramcontent.com/pod-product-compliance
Lightning Source LLC
Chambersburg PA
CBHW072151290526
45794CB00004B/1483